Balance for Ballad

Moon-J

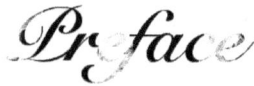

Balance is one of the most important elements in our lives as well as in design. In Asia, harmony and balance have been treated an ultimate way of life, and honored as the most valuable virtue. Therefore, I think it is very useful to review the definition of balance in Art. That is the reason why I create and publish these artworks.

I focused on several points before I created each piece.
1. The Weight: Each art piece has its own weight, so I composed two pieces together over one background along with measuring its weight in order to produce a new well-balanced artwork. The result will be a 'three as one' in harmony.
2. Composition with coiled lines: A line of each piece is constructed on a background to build a space where shows the multiple dimension as one.
3. Ballad: It is about memories and added a poetic form about emotions that all humans can have.

Moon-J, a day in 2022.

Balance: about its weight

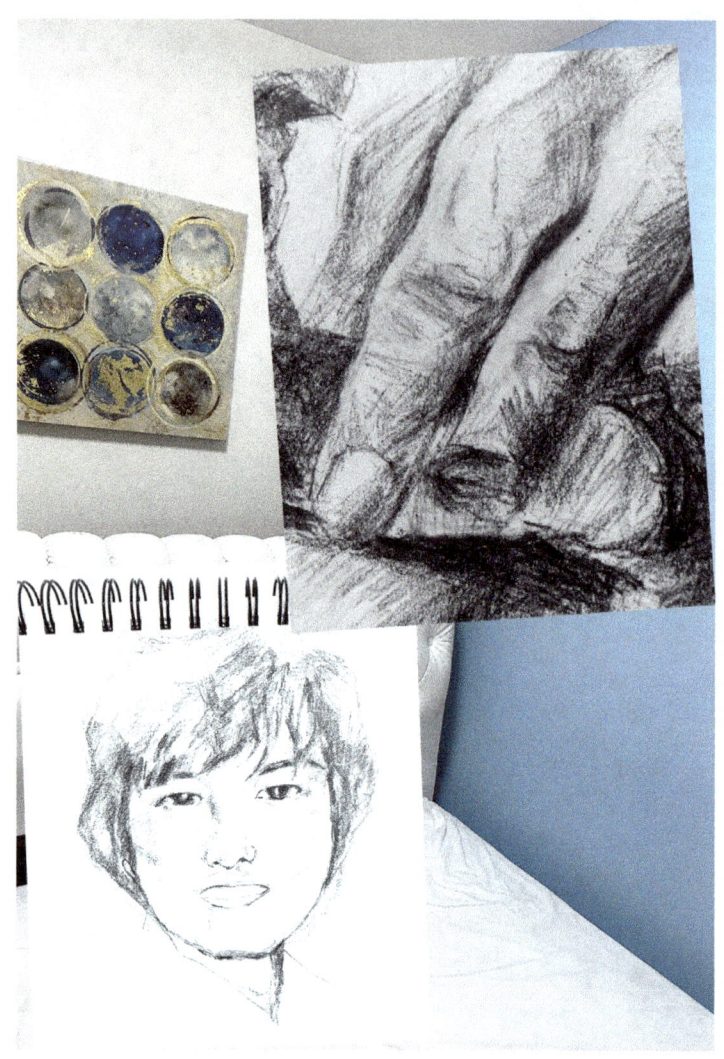

B-1. 2022.

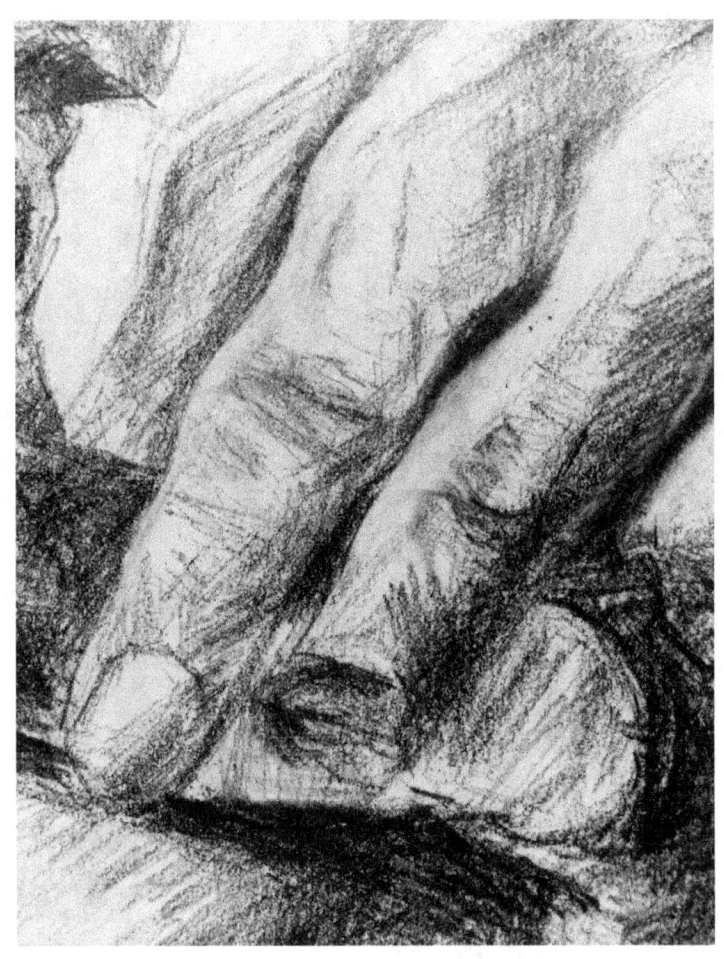

Lost Love. Pencil. 2012.
When you left me,
even all my blood flowing stopped.

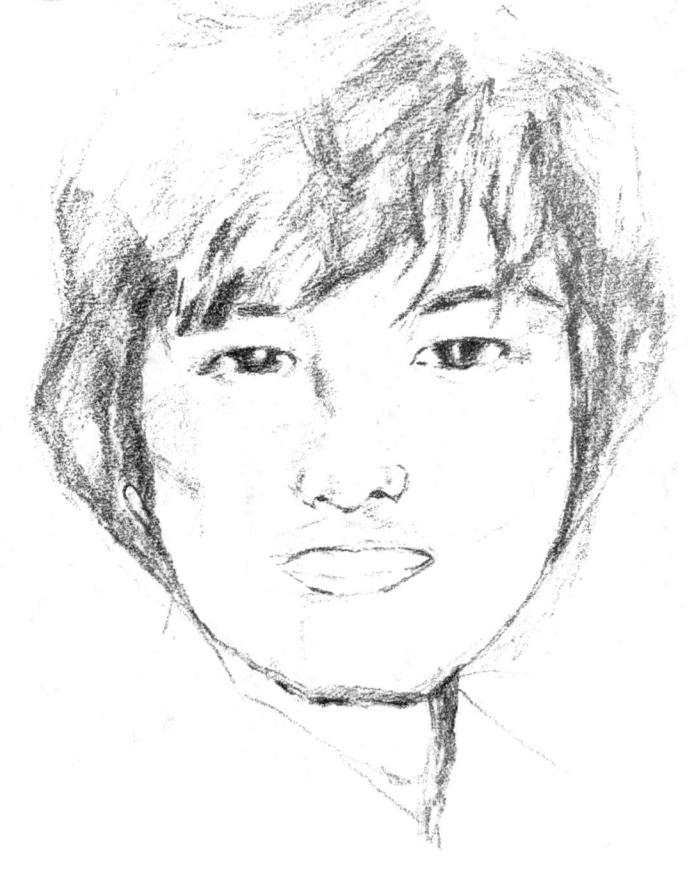

I called it Love. Pencil. 2019.

LOVE

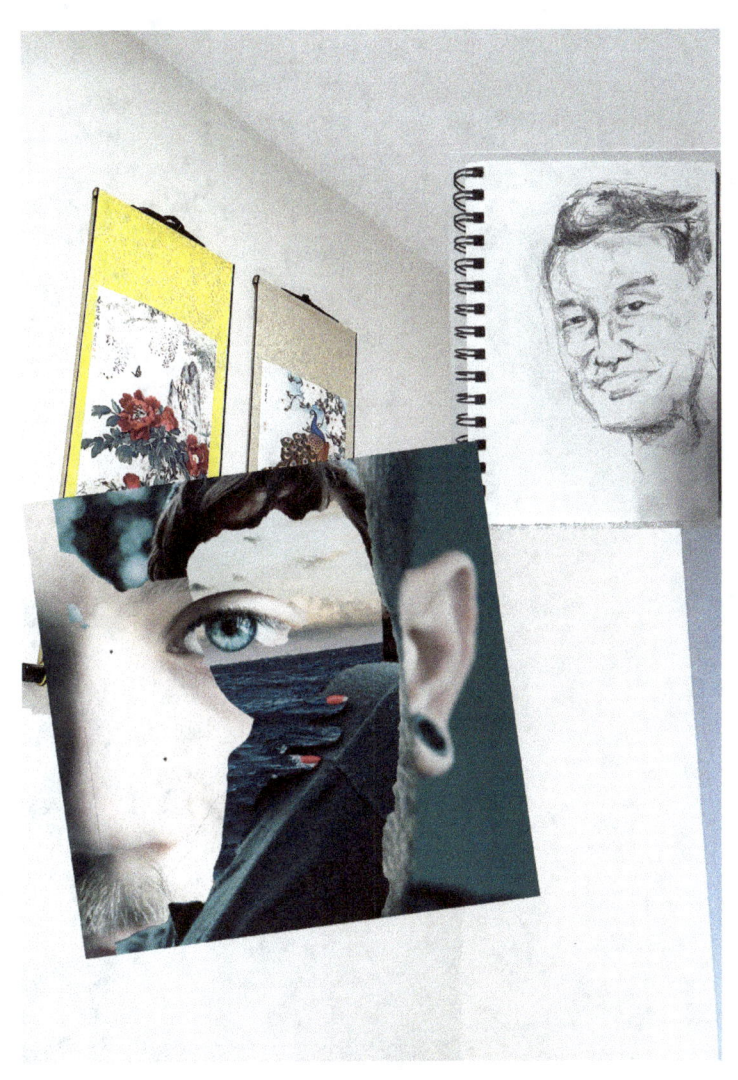

B-2. 2021.

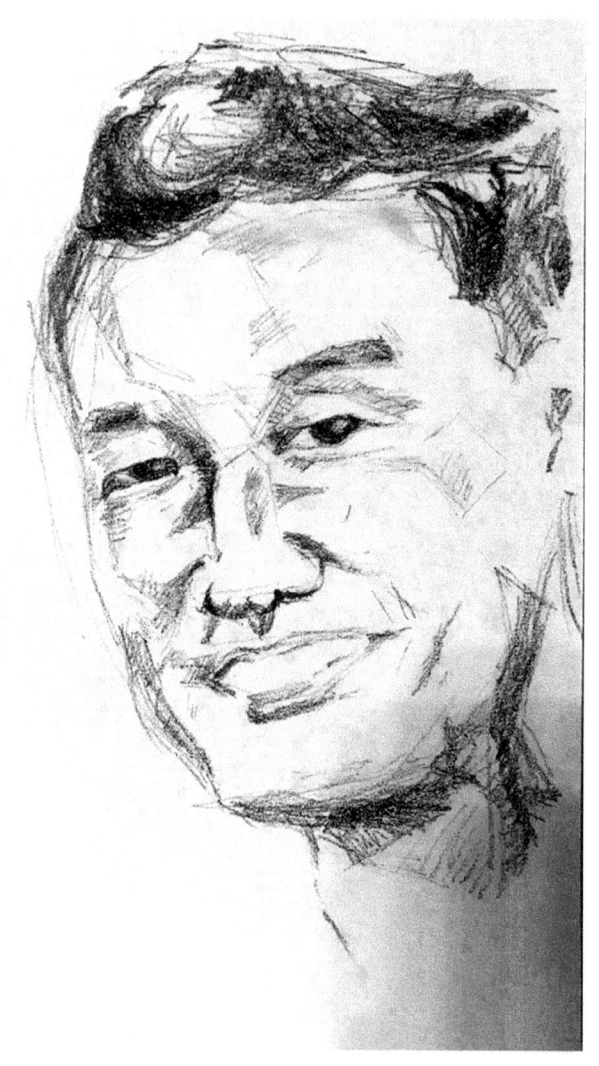

Someone. Pencil. 2019.
When I saw someone,
he became someone special to me.
When I called him, he became a memory.

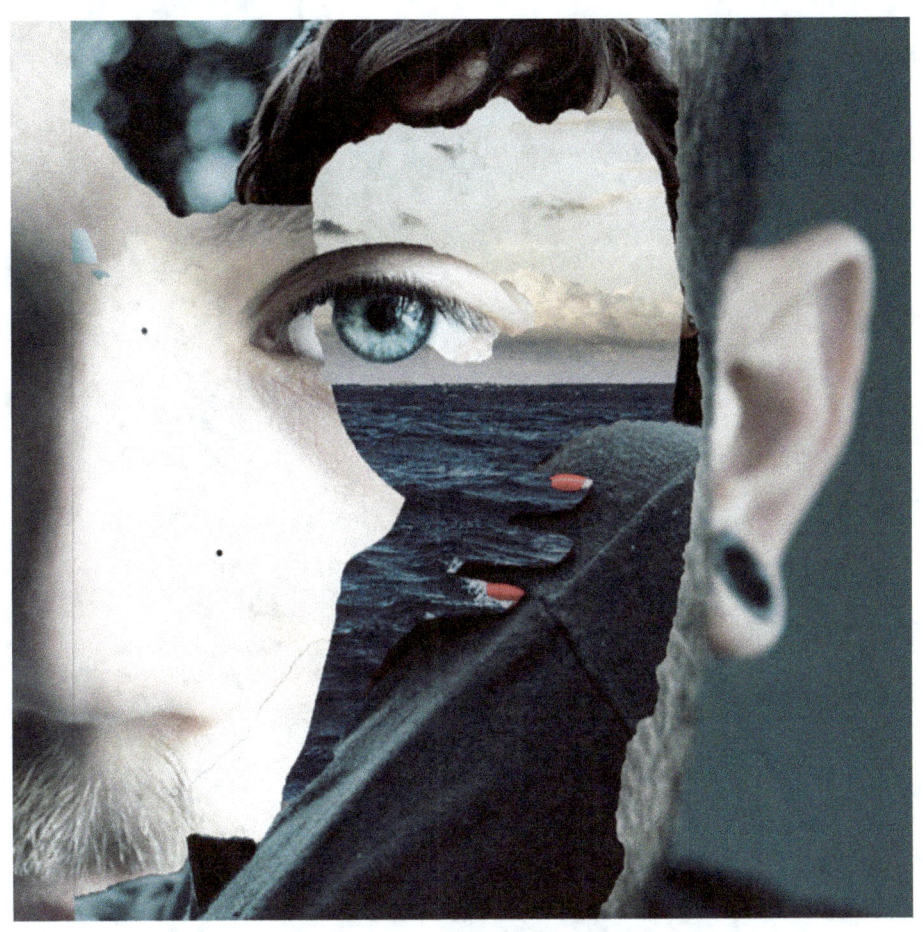

Chaos. Adobe Photoshop. 2019.
                                             Memories are like that.

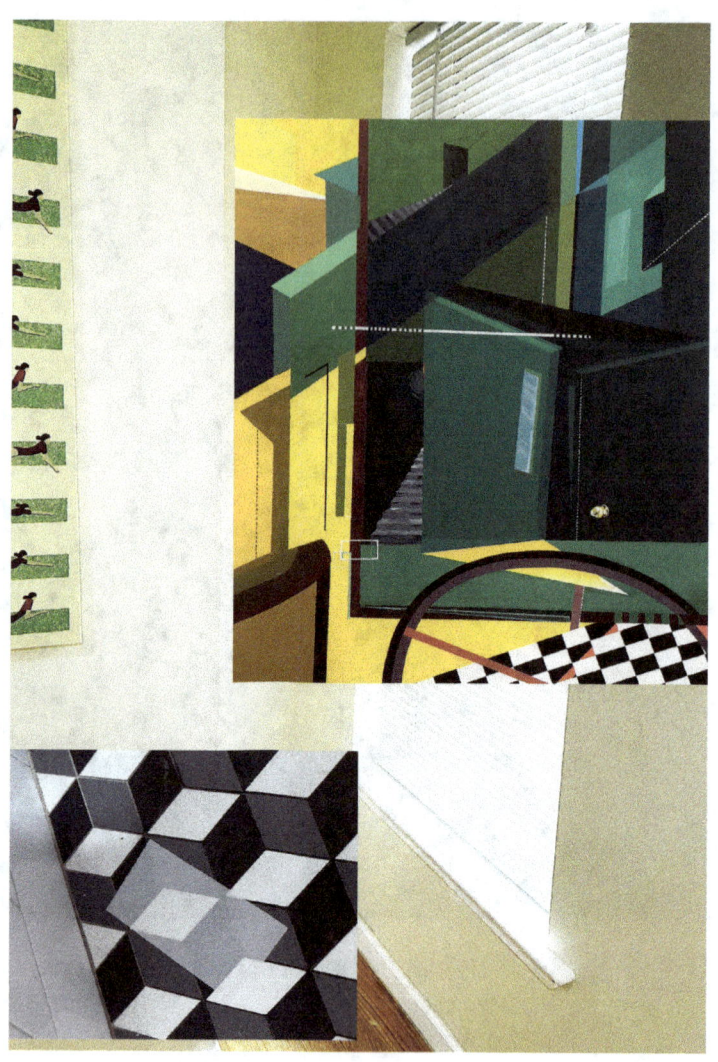

B-3. 2021.

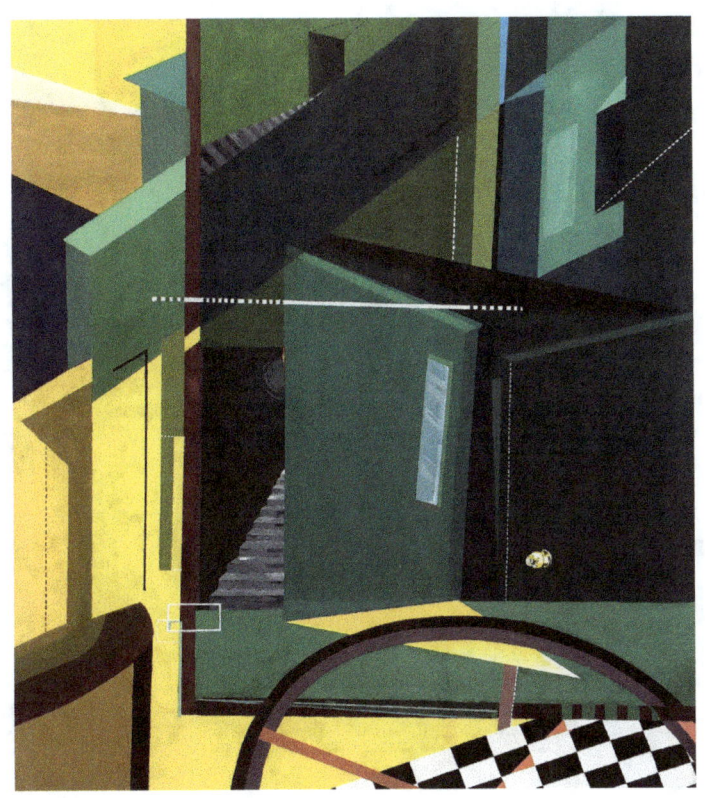

Maze. Acrylic. 2017.
There was a city out the window.

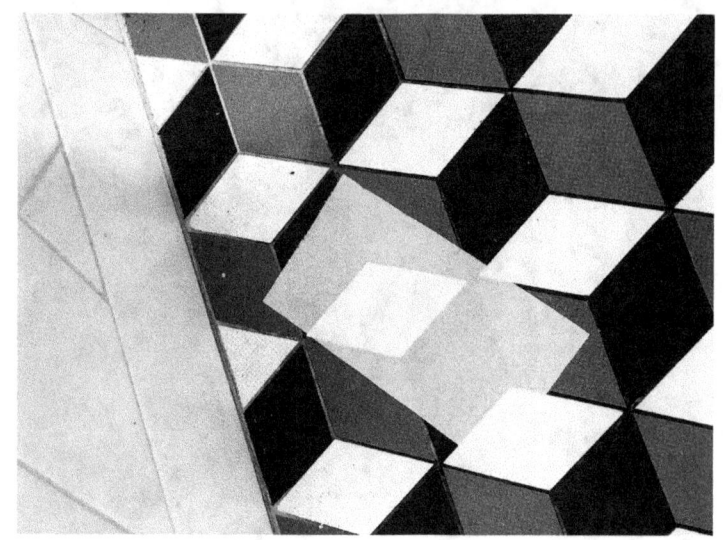

Toilet Paper. Photo. 2018.
Attacked.

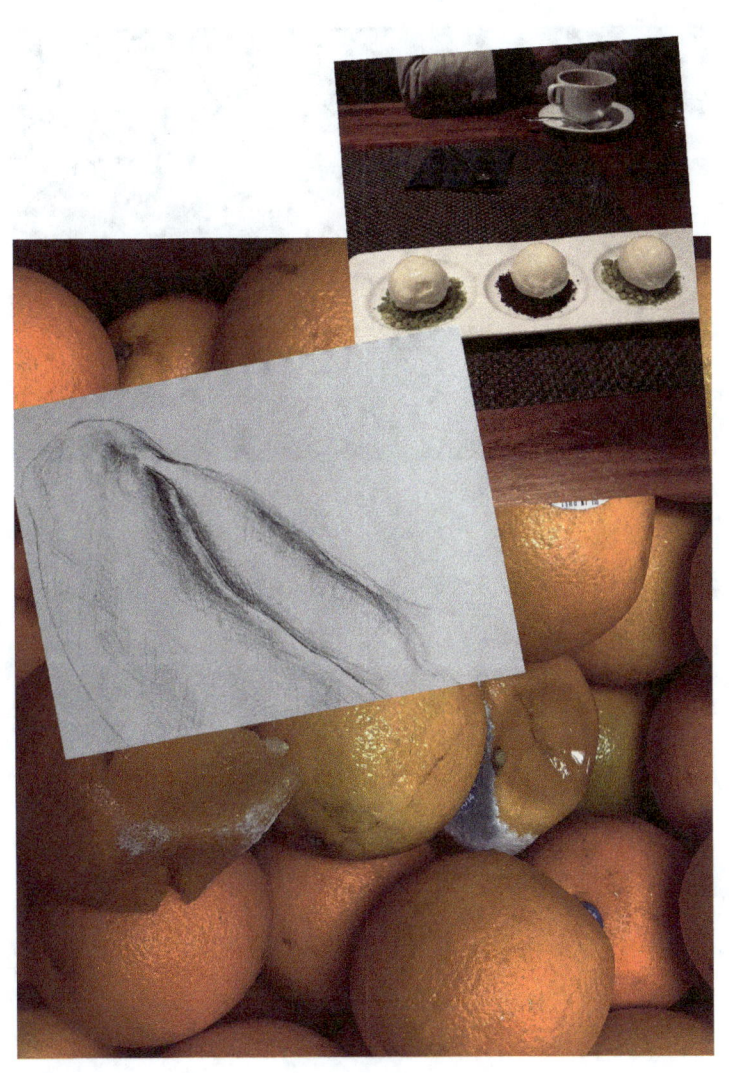

B-4. 2021.

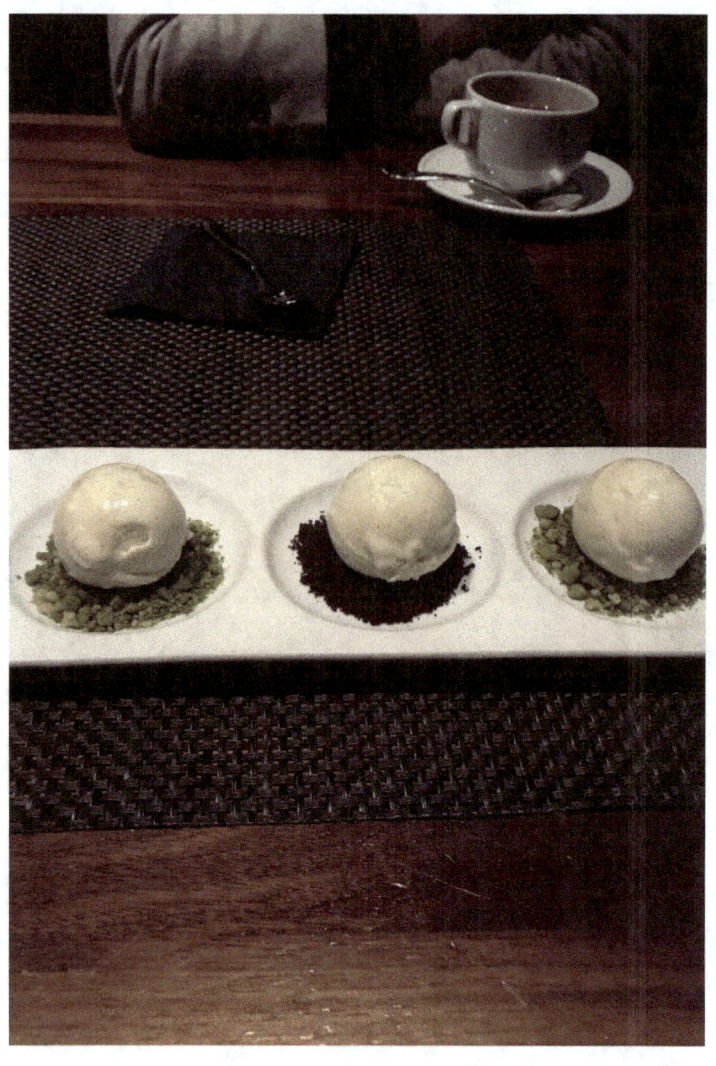

Three Scoops of Ice cream. Photo. 2019.
Ice Cream in January.

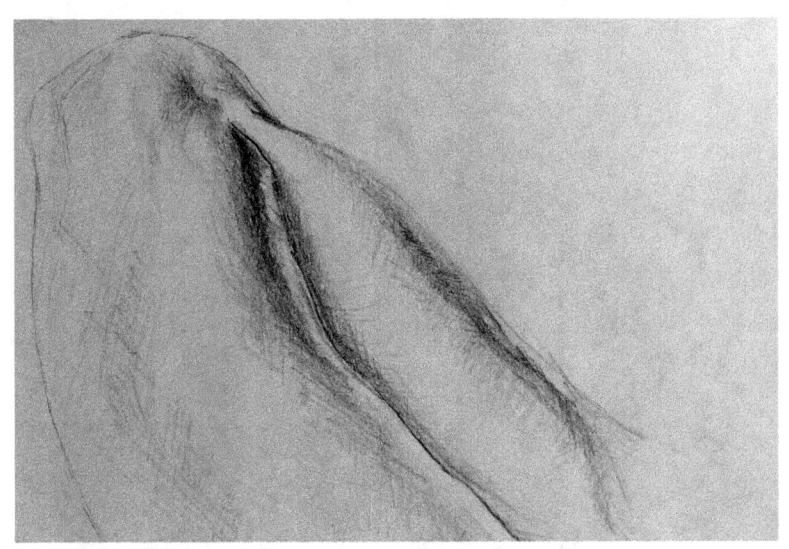

Thigh. Pencil. 2014.

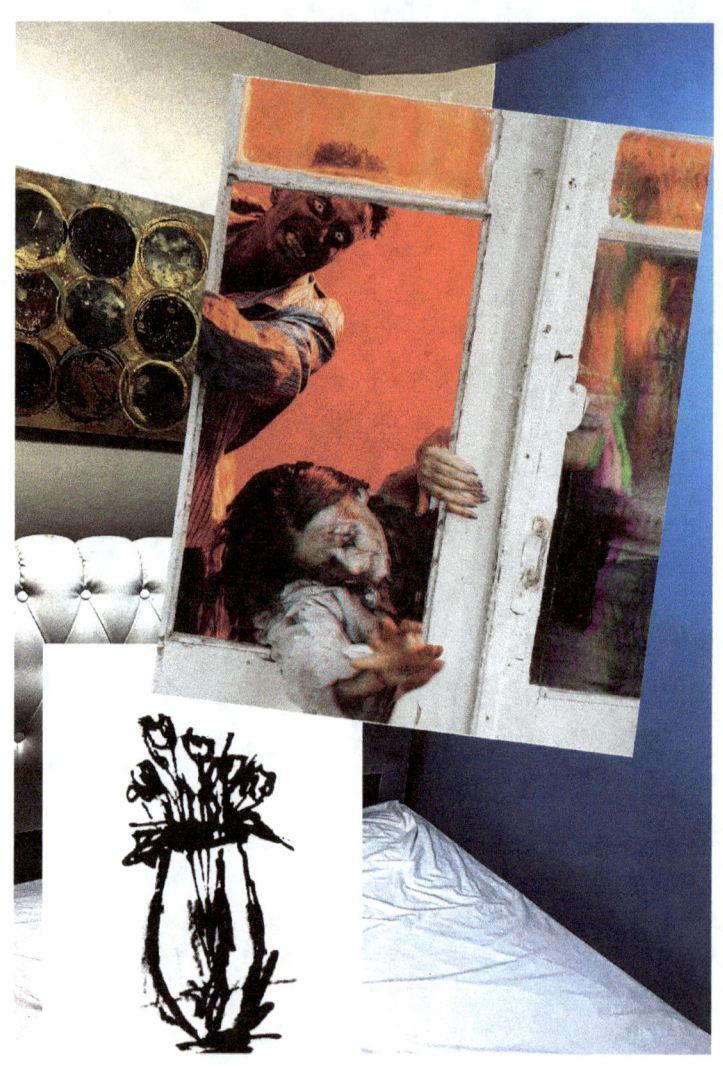

B-5. 2021.

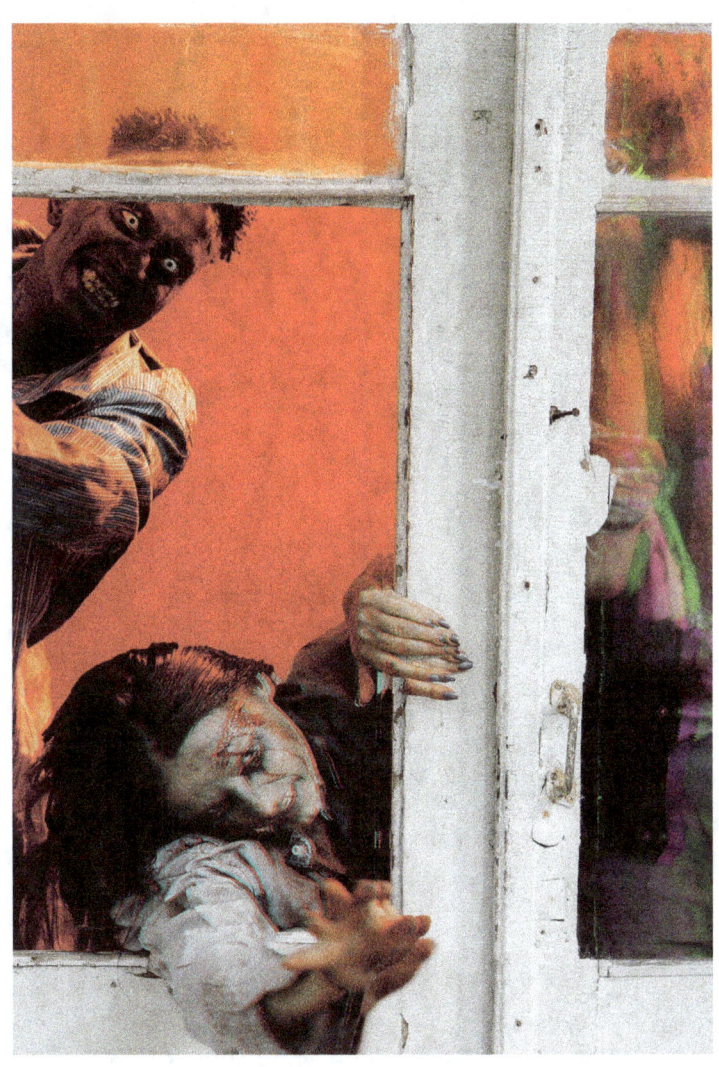

Untitled. Adobe Photoshop. 2019.
When someone calls you,
You will be Love or Death.

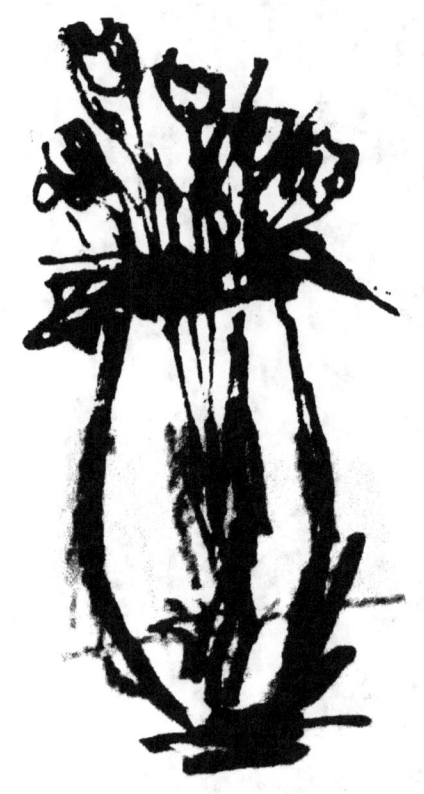

Flower Pot. Pen&Adobe Photoshop. 2016.
Flowers flower.

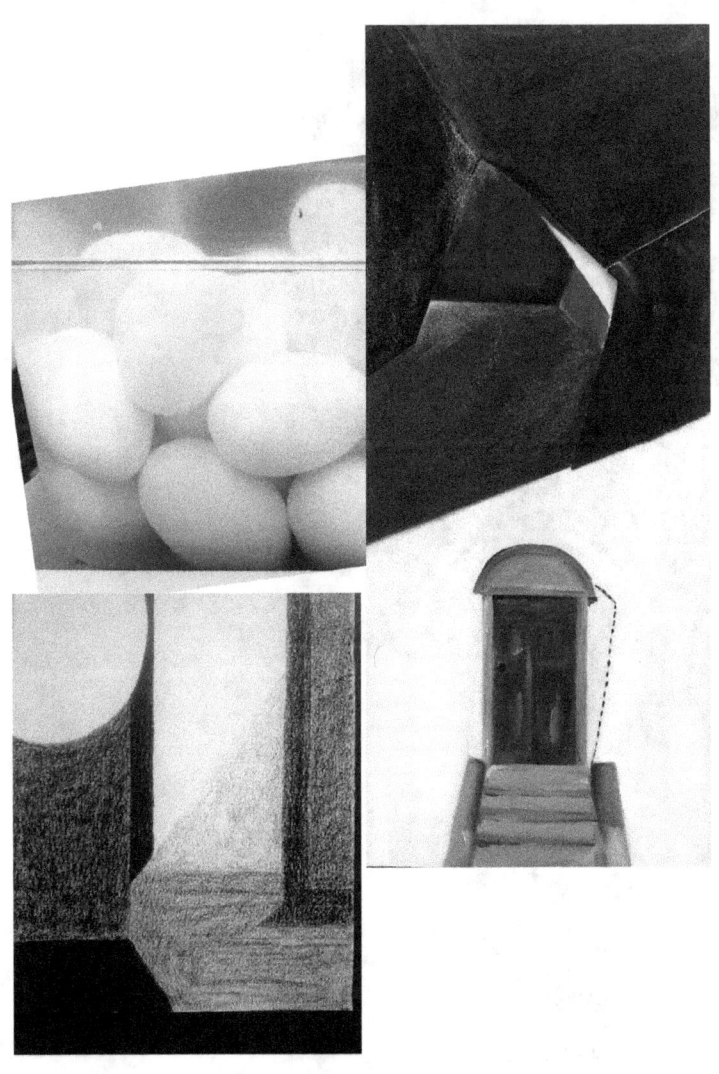

B-6. 2021.

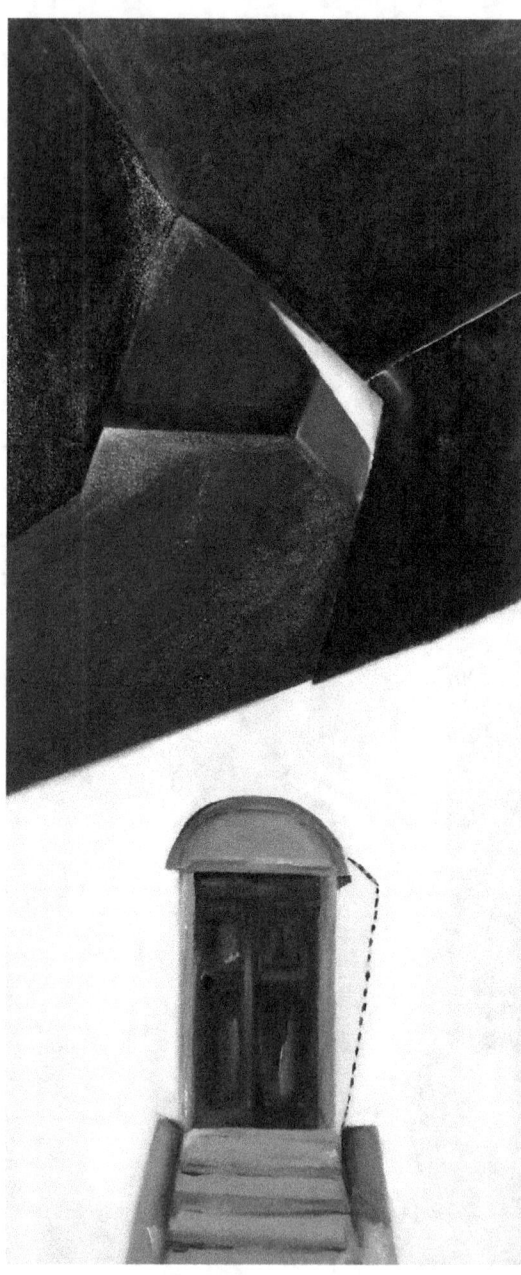

Untitled. Acrylic. 2017.

When you open the door, there will be a way to another space.

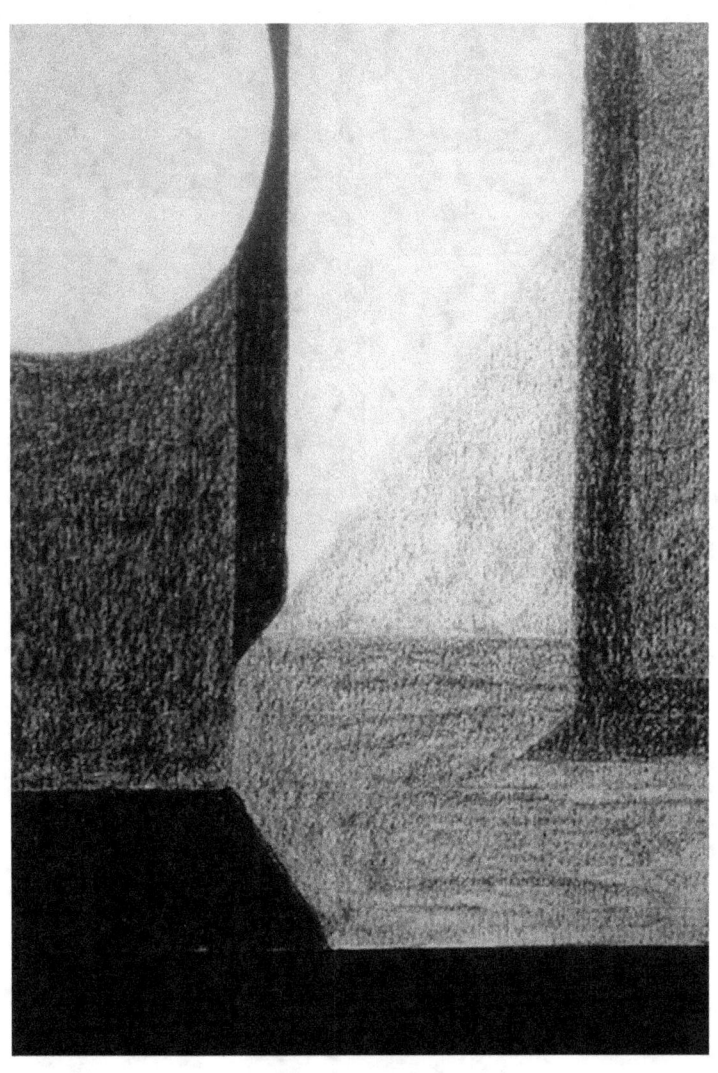

Untitled. Charcoal. 2014.
A world composed with a light & shadow.

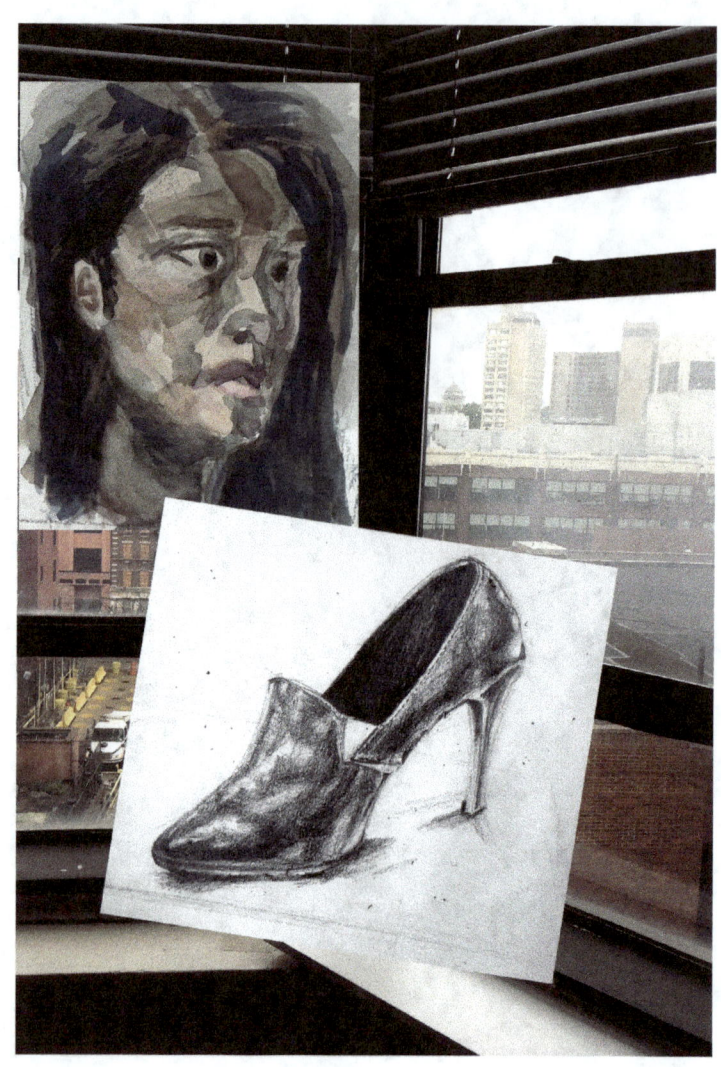

B-7. 2022.

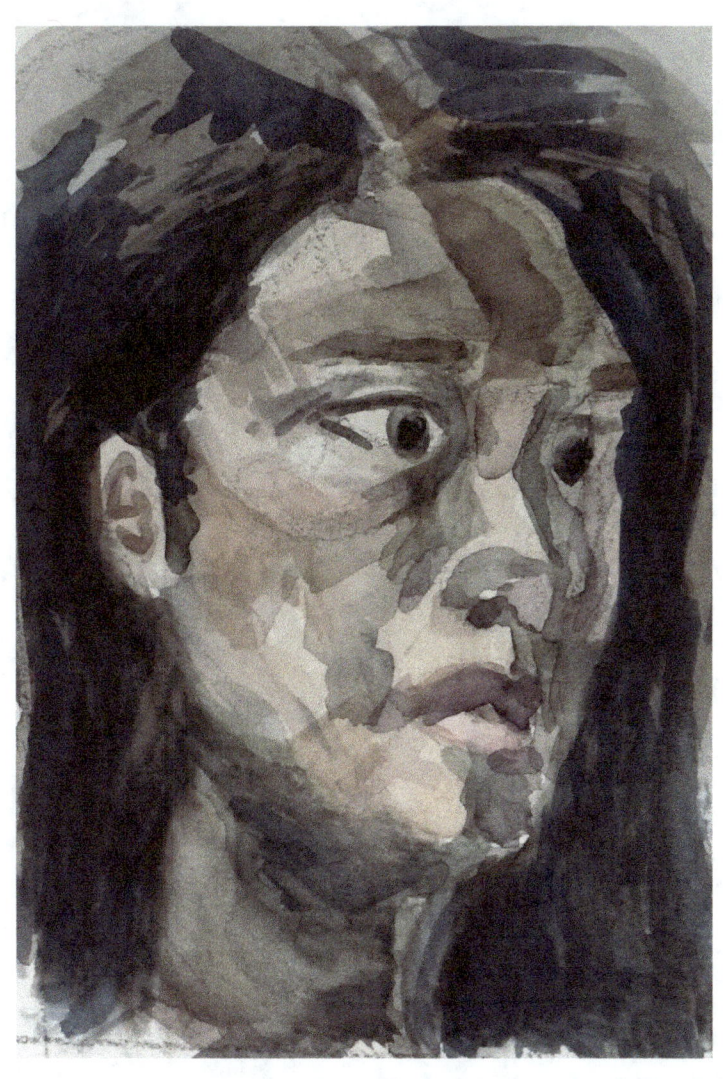

Untitled. Watercolor. 2016.
I am looking at you.

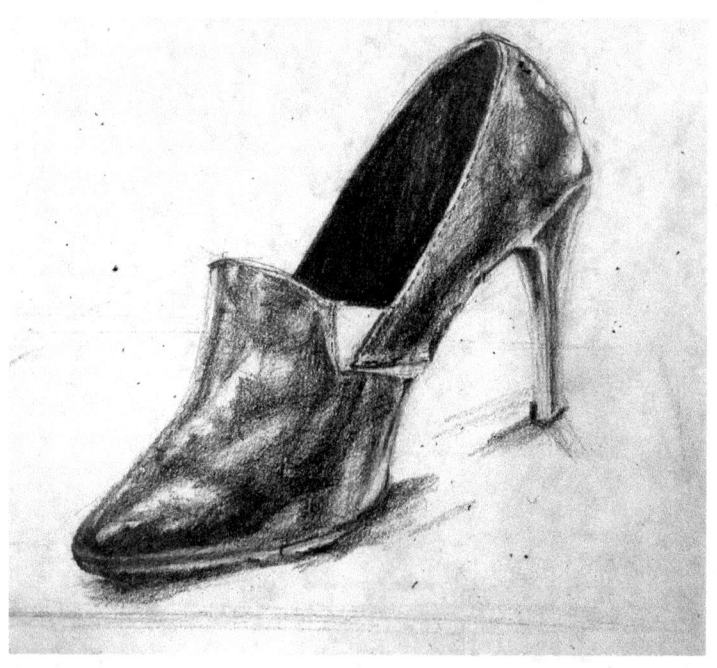

High Heel. Pencil. 2015.
If I can meet you again, I will wear a high heel.

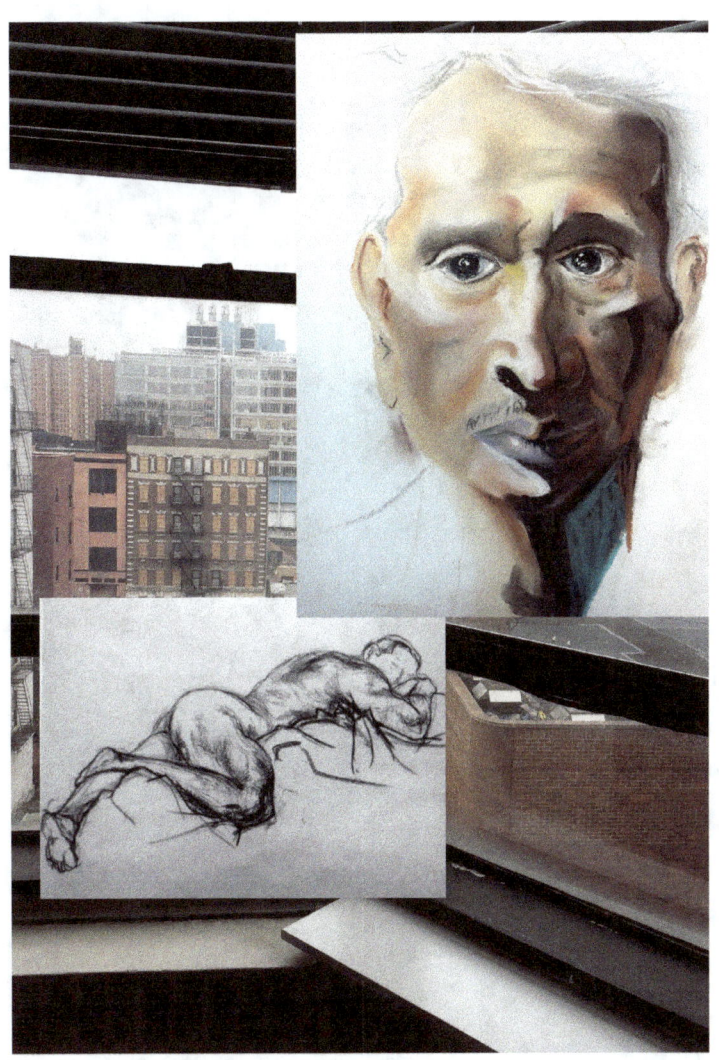

B-8. 2022.

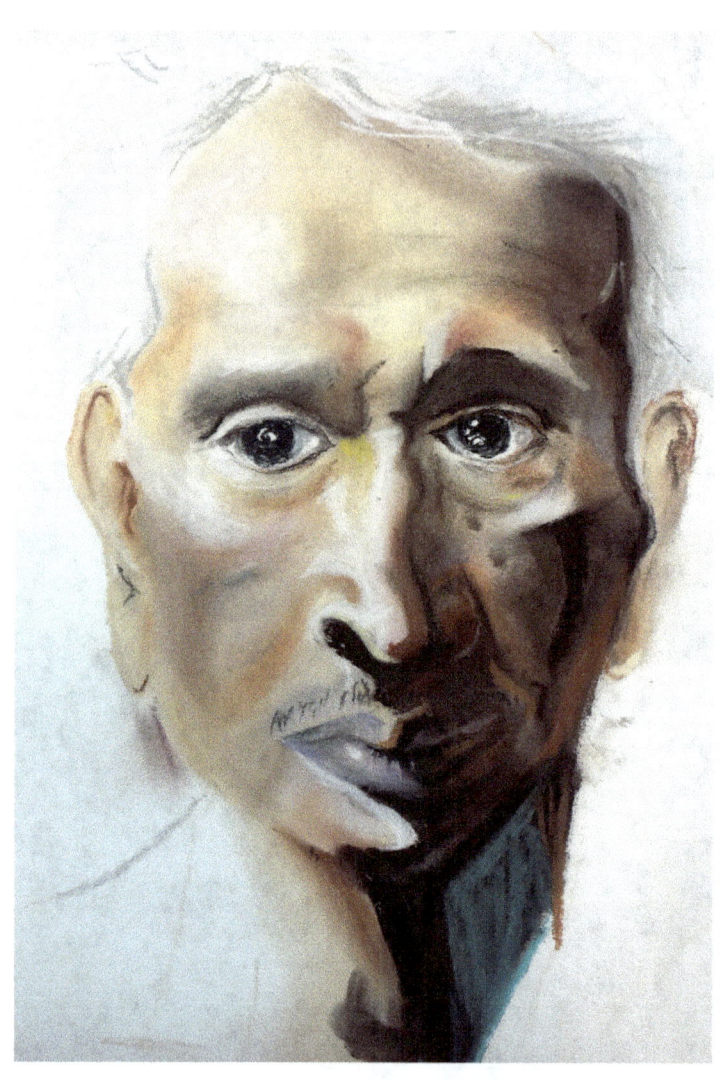

Caesar. Pastel. 2015.
My old friend, hope you would live long.

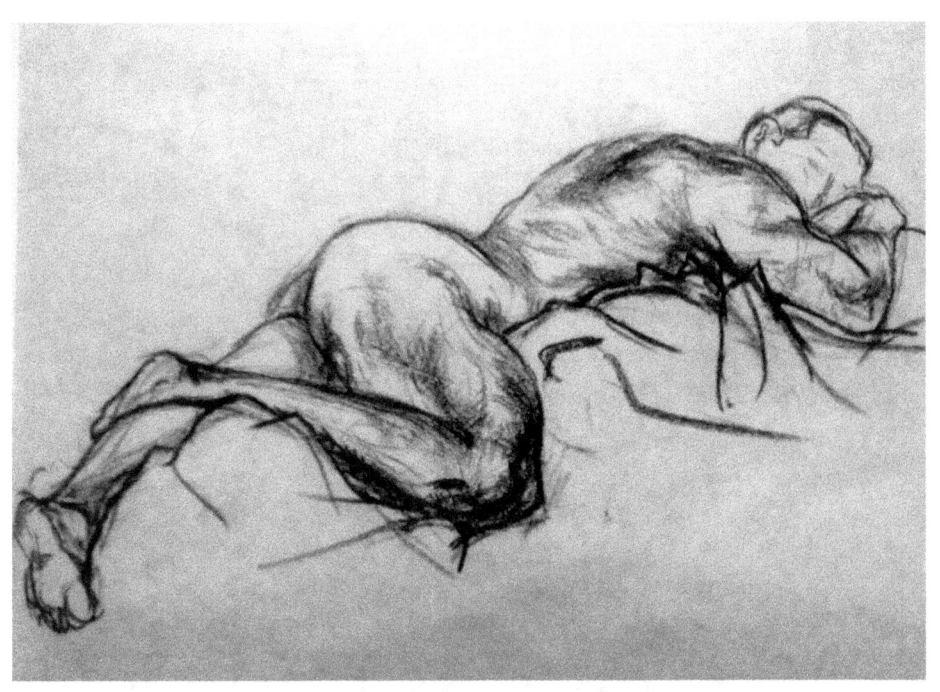

Nude. Charcoal. 2013.
Life is too short. Youth is already behind me.

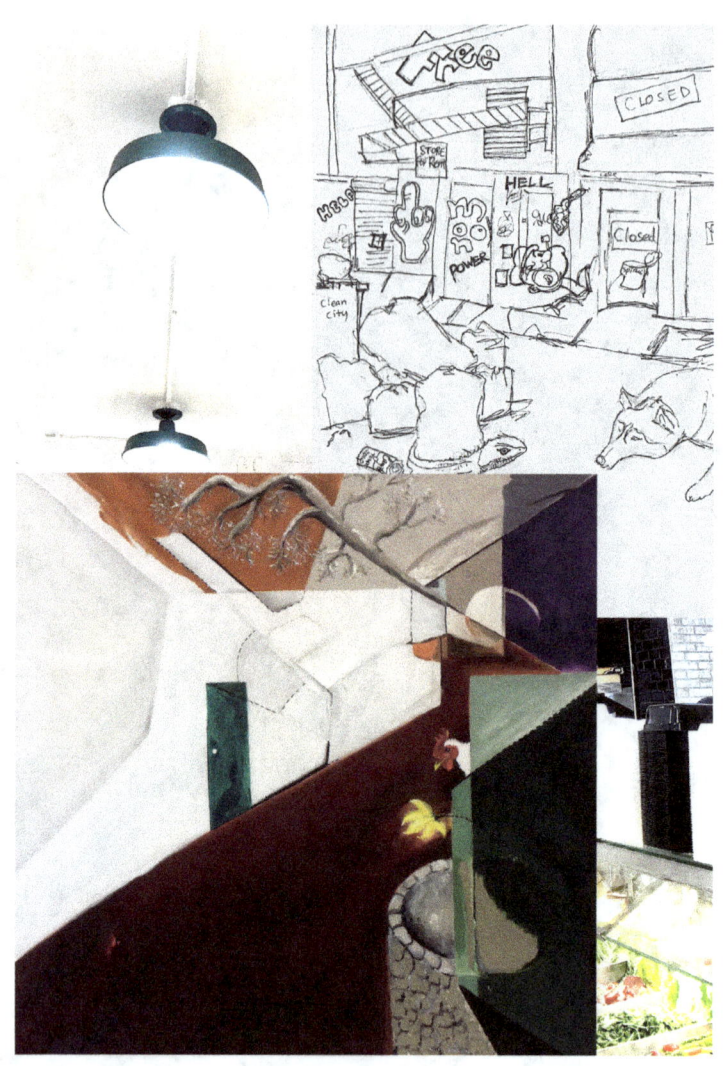

B-9. 2021.

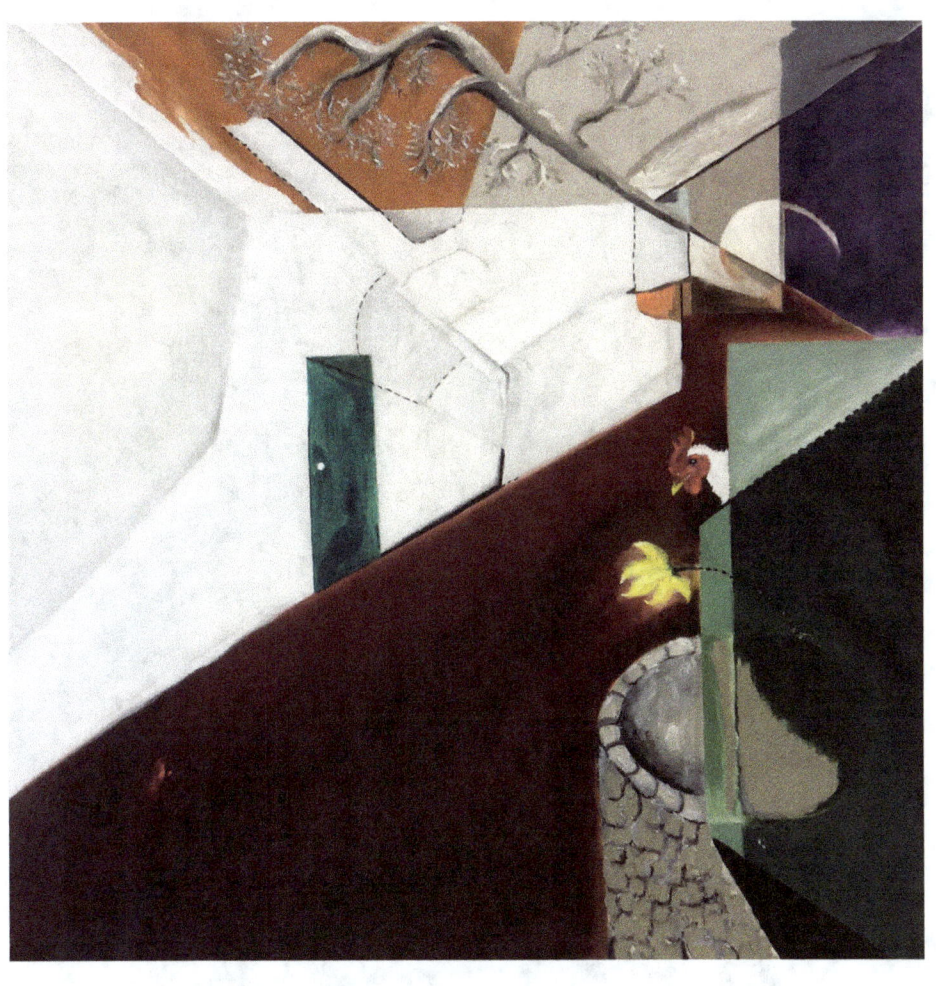

In my youth. Oil. 2014.
My grandmother and grandfather lived there,
and they took care of me.
They are living in the heaven now.

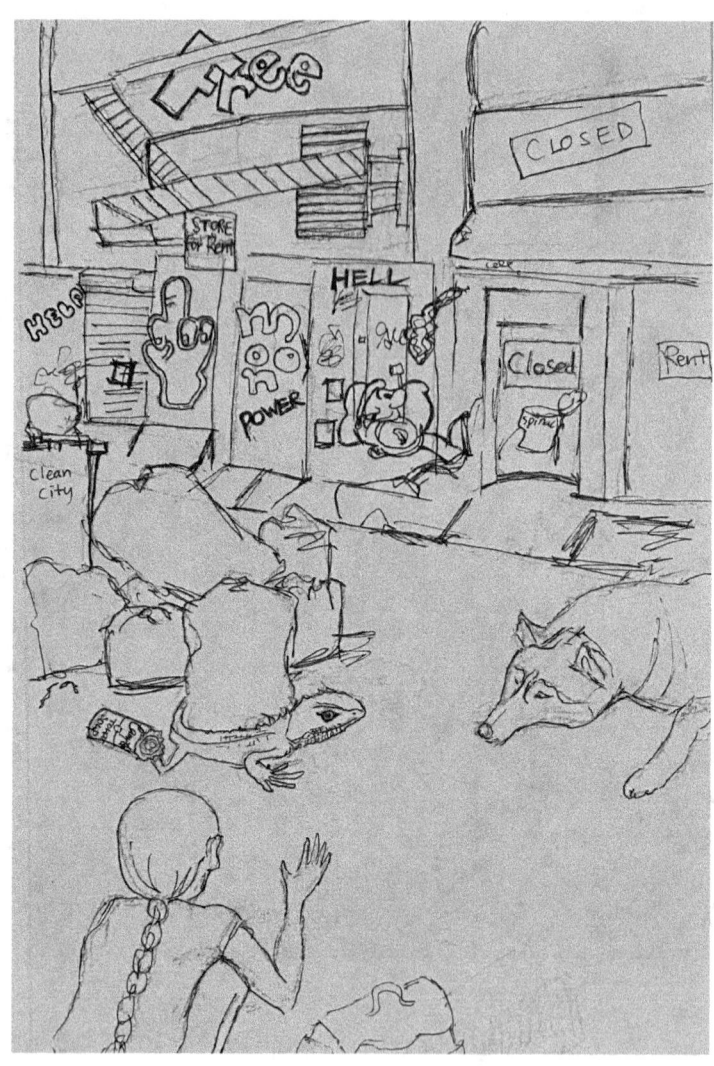

Save the lizard. Pen. 2020.
Dark side of the big city.
Someone becomes a hero, a created hero.

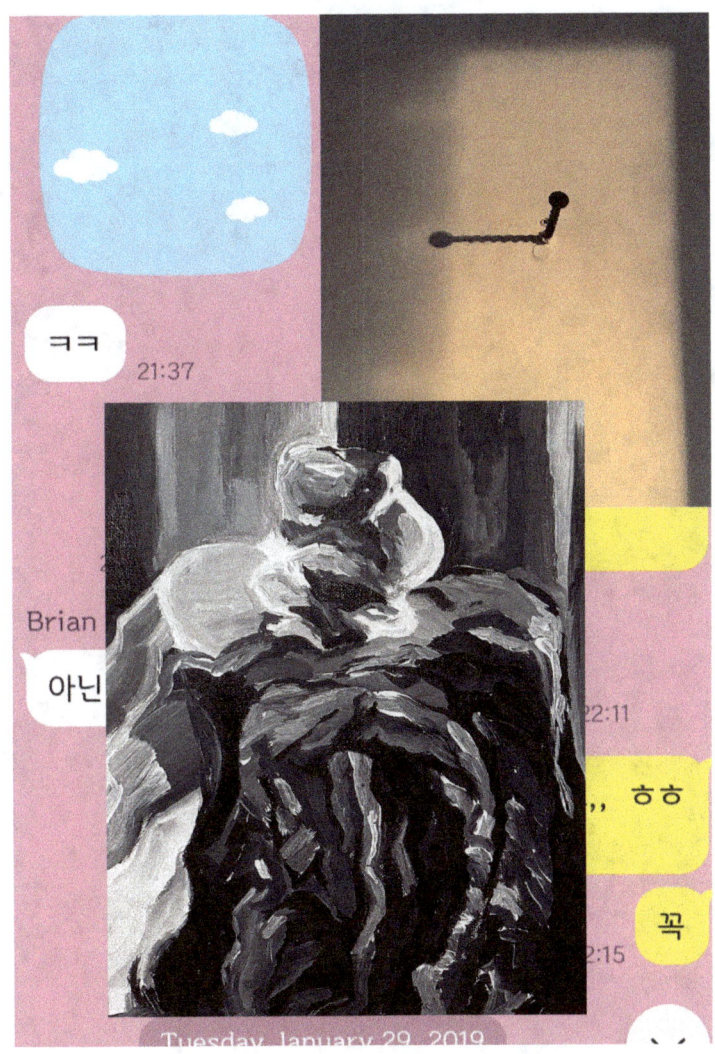

B-10. 2021.

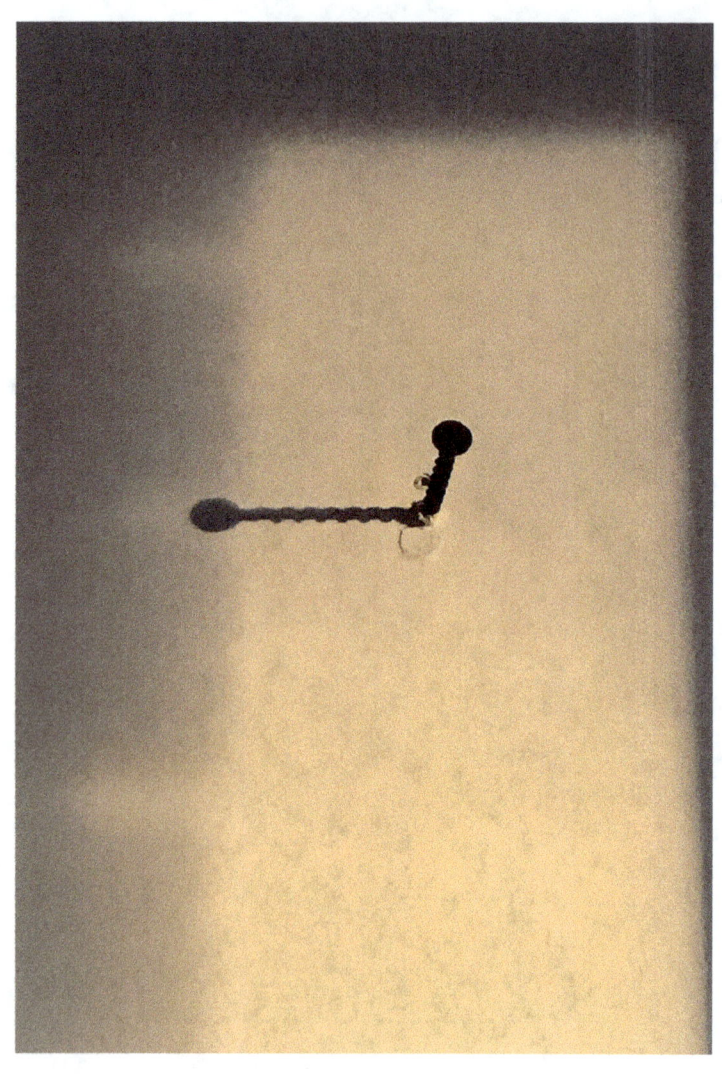

Hurt. Photo. 2015.
You and my heart.

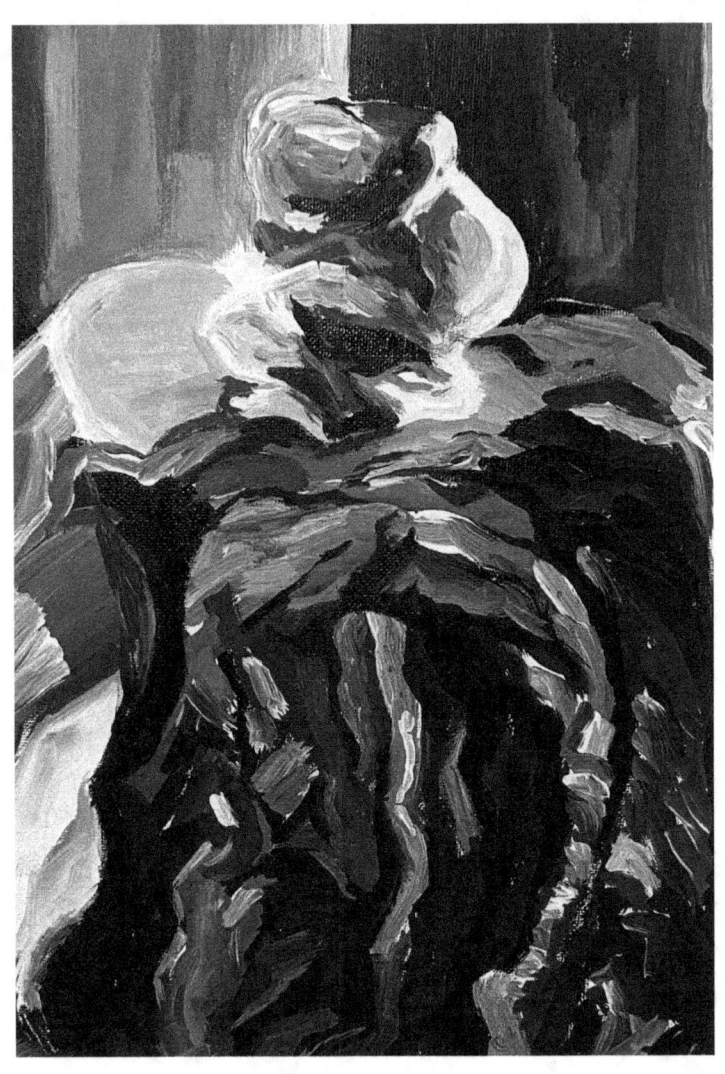

Untitled. Acrylic. 2015.
I am crying over you.

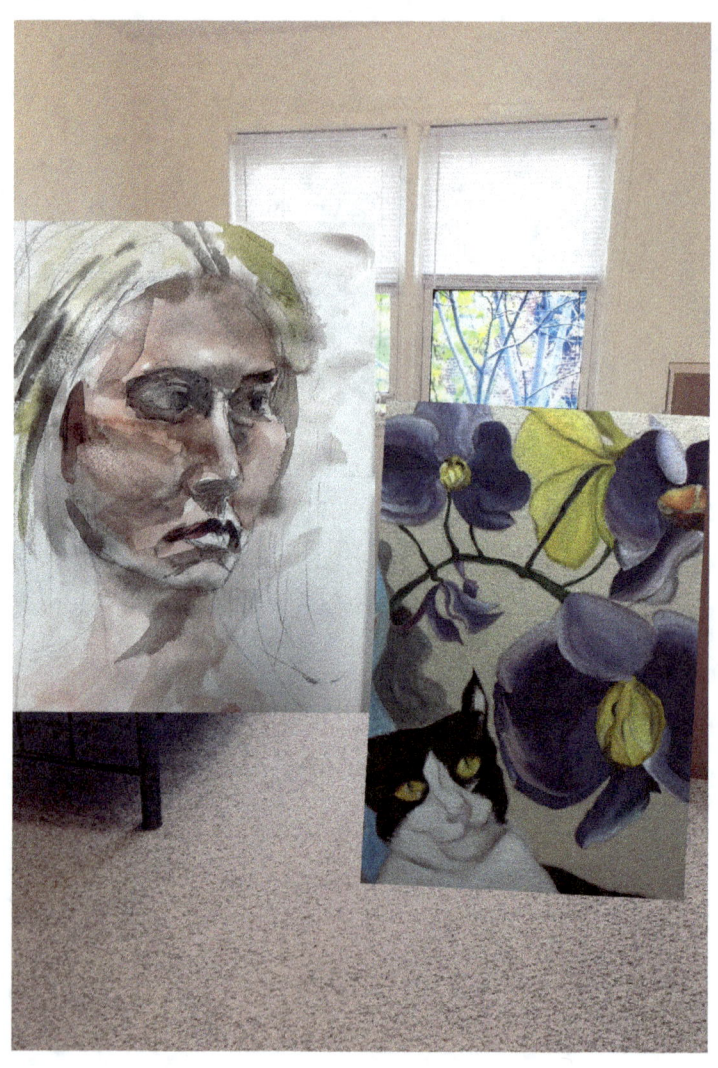

B-11. 2022.

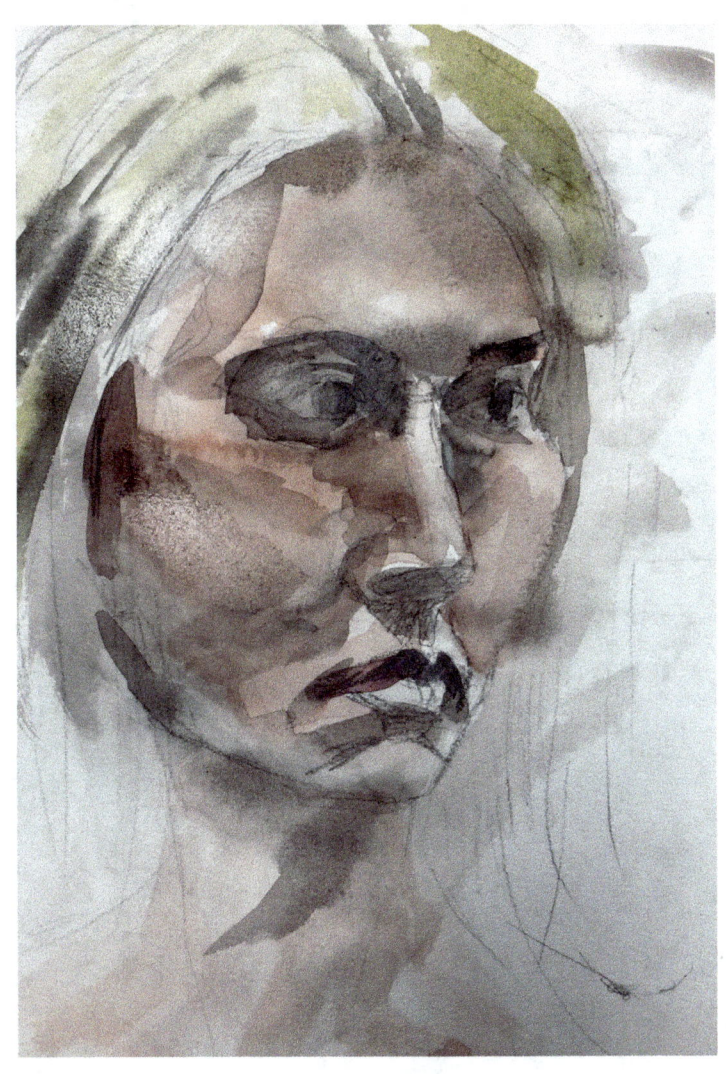

A girl. Watercolor. 2016.
My life is not finished yet.

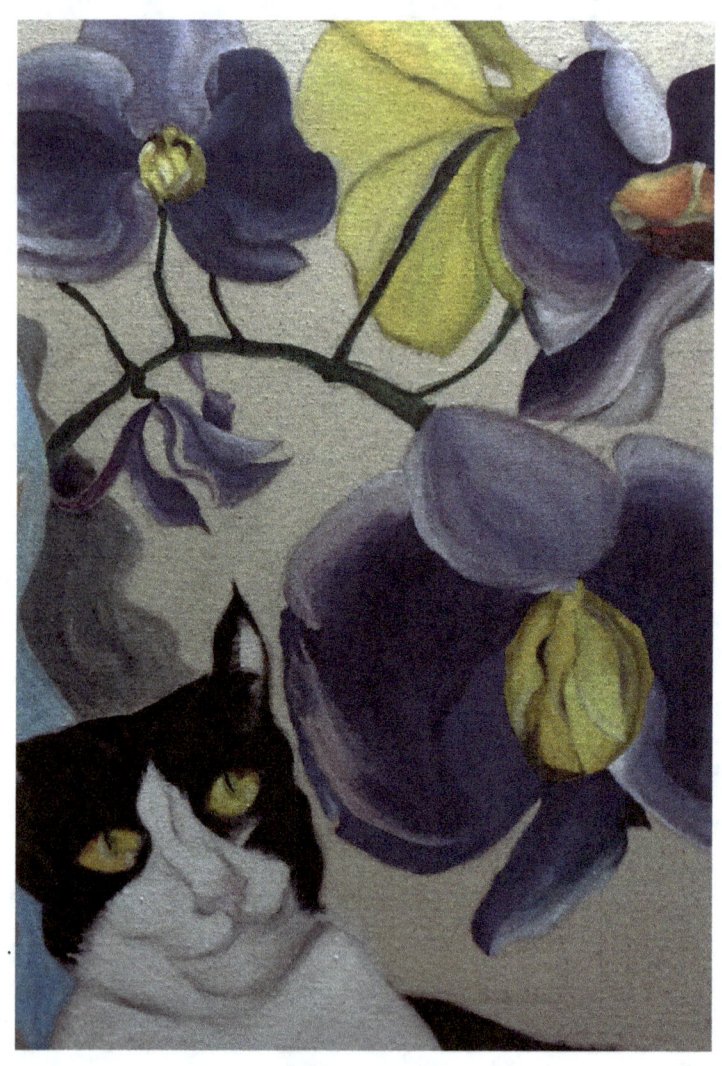

A cat in Spring. Acrylic. 2014.
Here is the spring again, You left me in that spring.

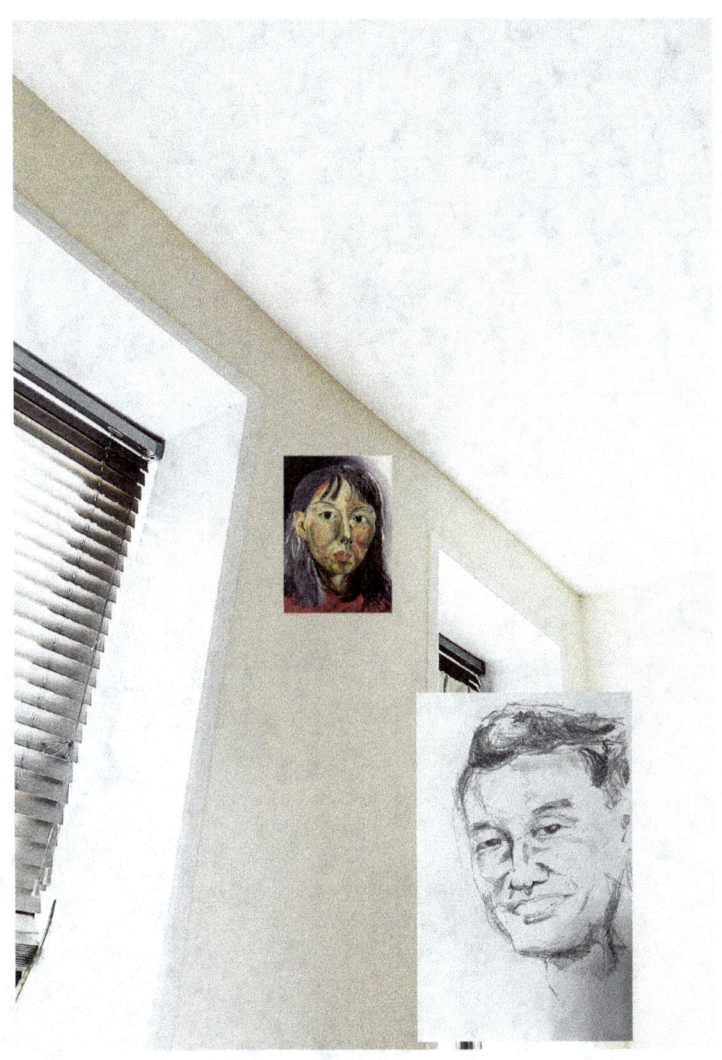

B-12. 2022.

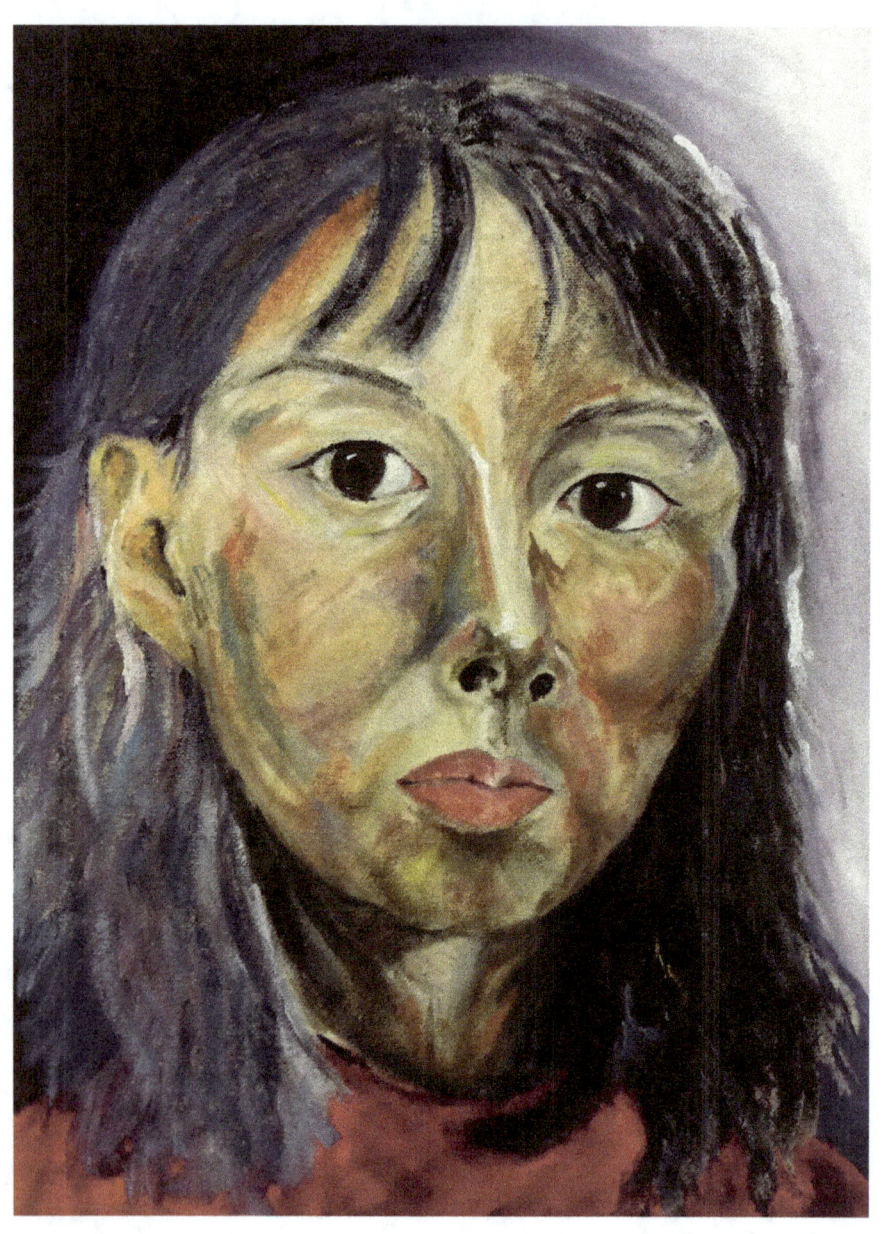

Self-Portrait. Oil. 2015.

I was born.

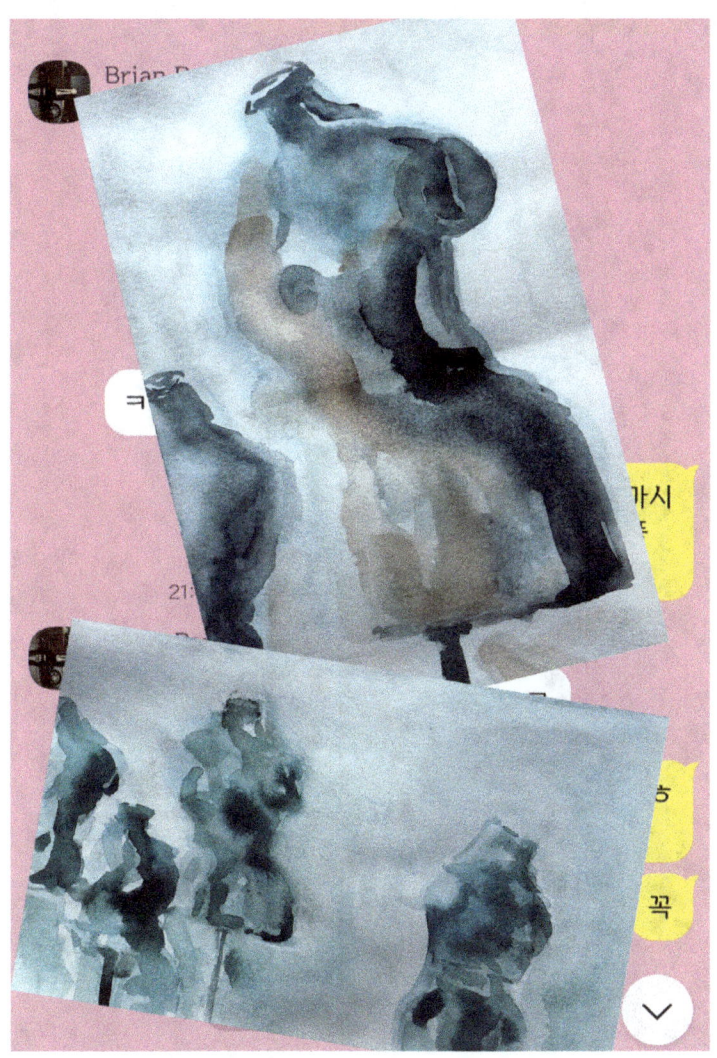

B-13. 2021.

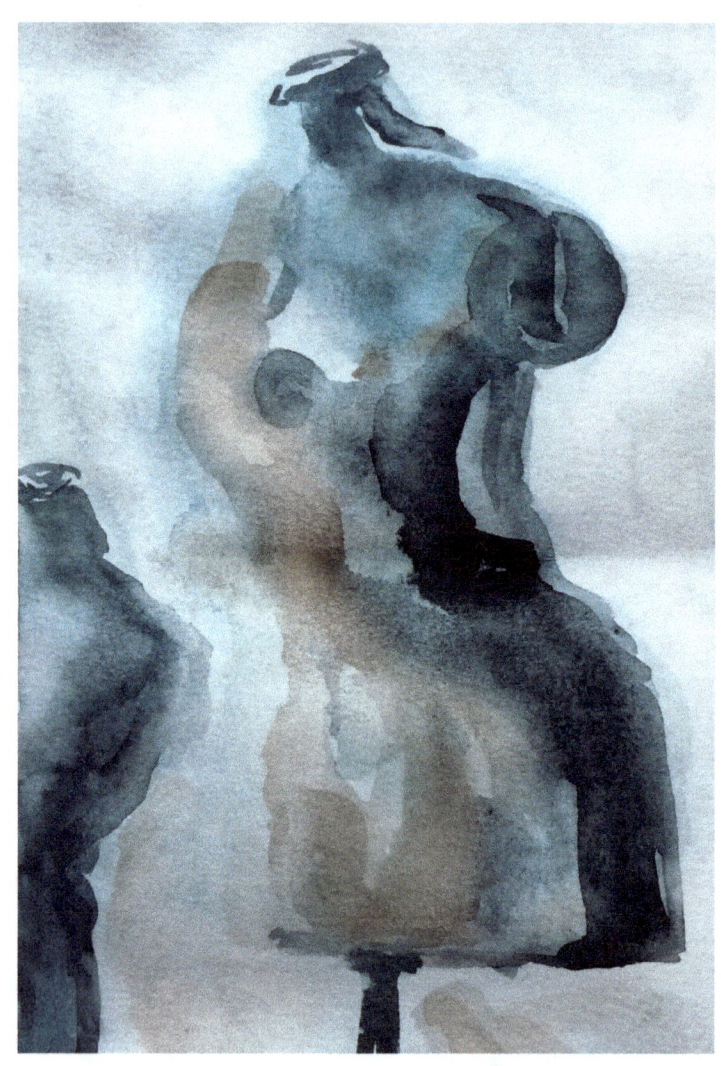

Mannequin. Watercolor. 2015.
If I fit you, are you gonna come back to me?

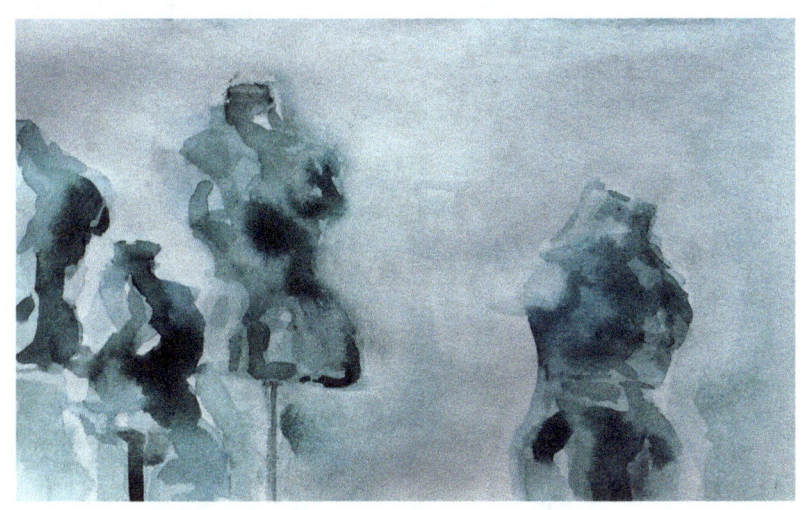

Mannequin2. Watercolor. 2015.

Still life. My life.

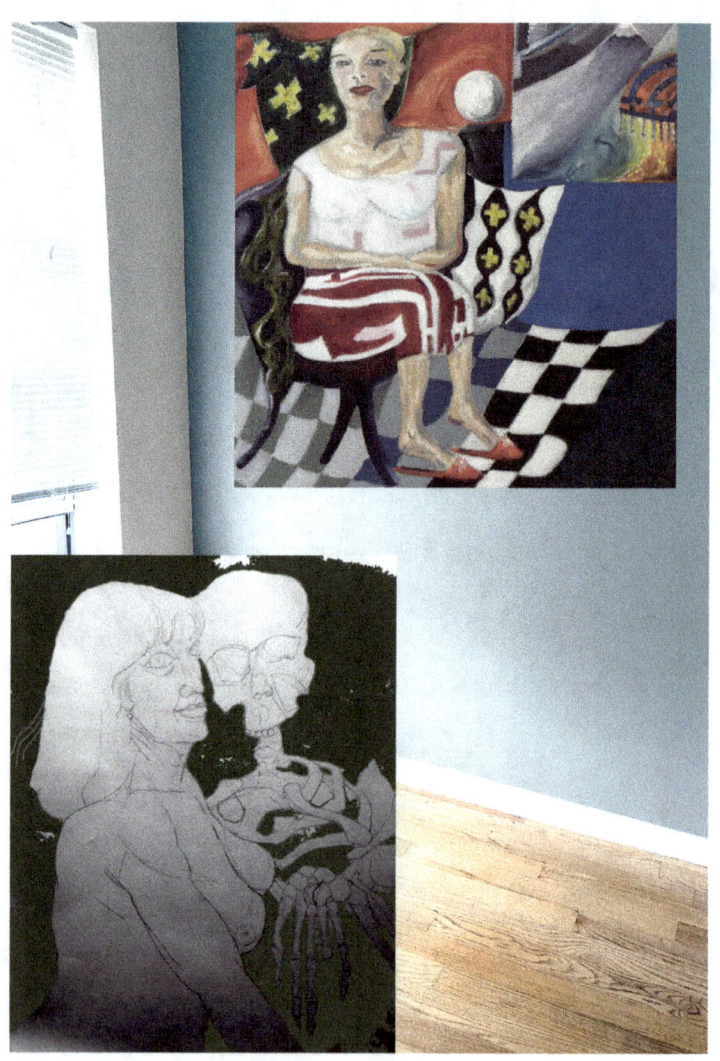

B-14. 2021.

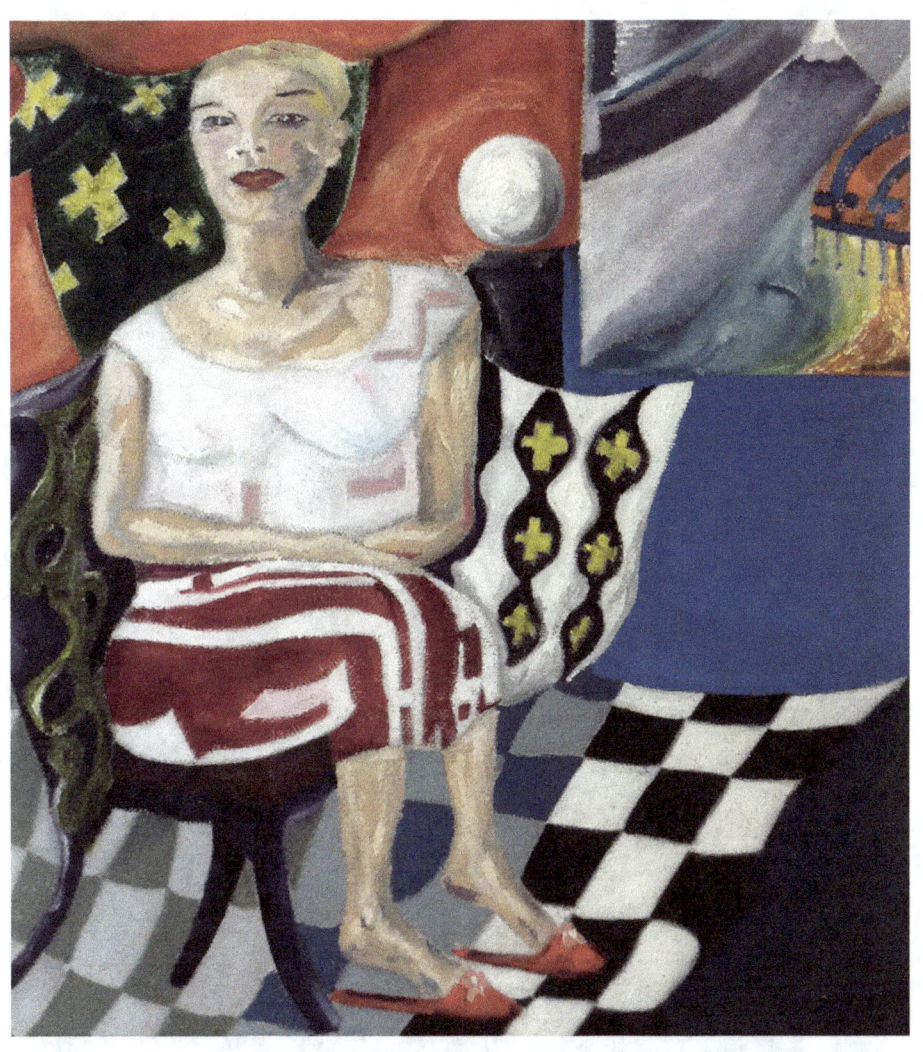

Untitled. Acrylic. 2014.
Magic Mt. My favorite noble.

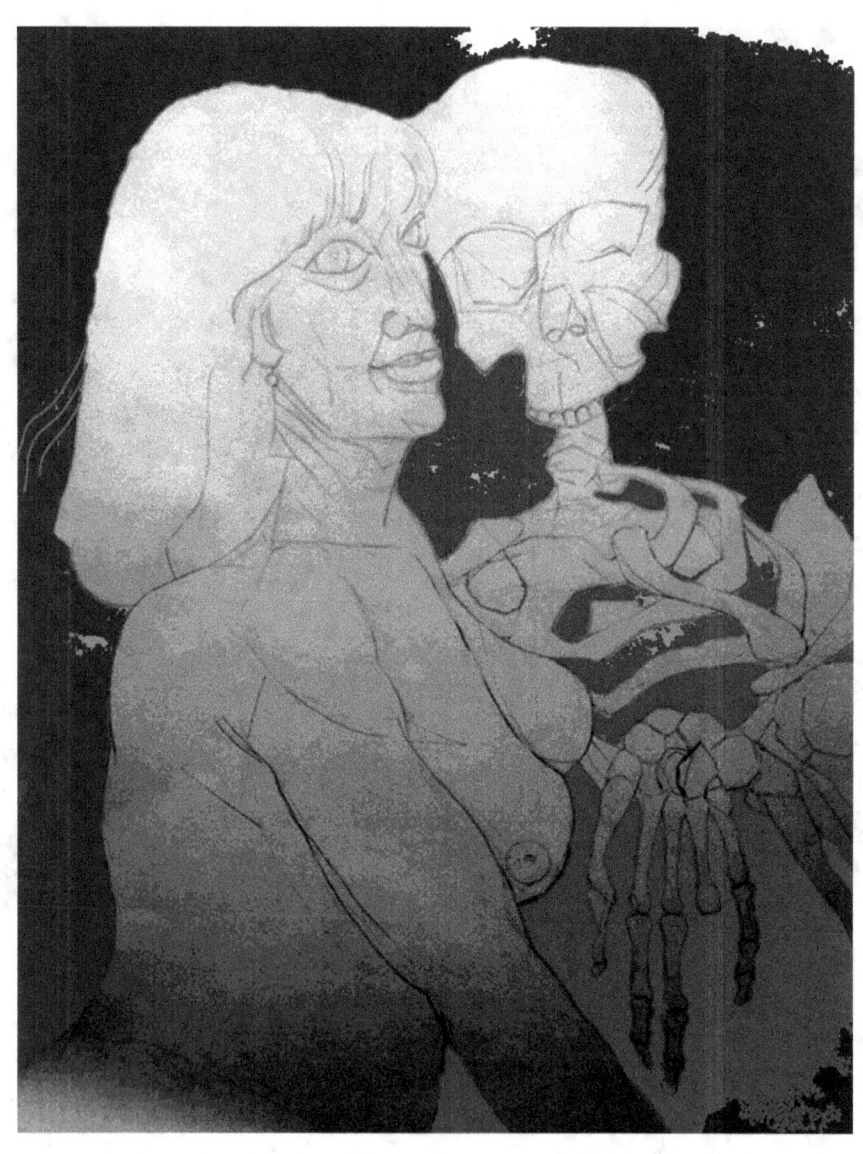

Life. Pencil & Adobe Photoshop. 2013.
No questionable.

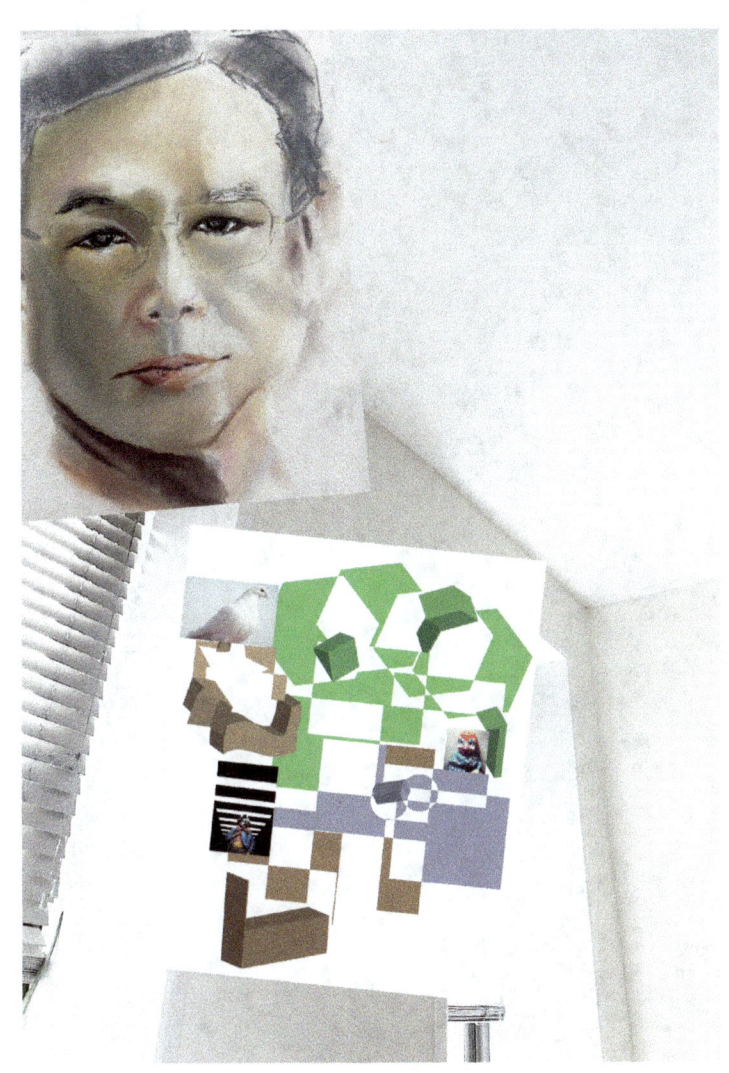

B-15. 2022.

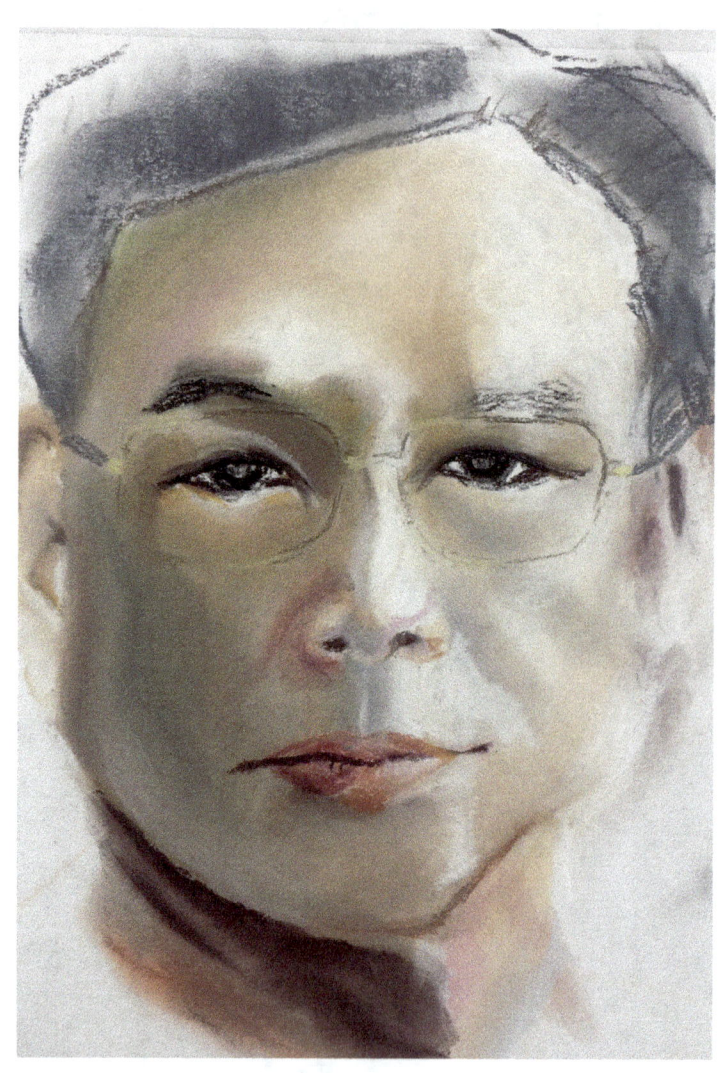

FATHER. Pastel. 2015.
Always Thank you & I love you.

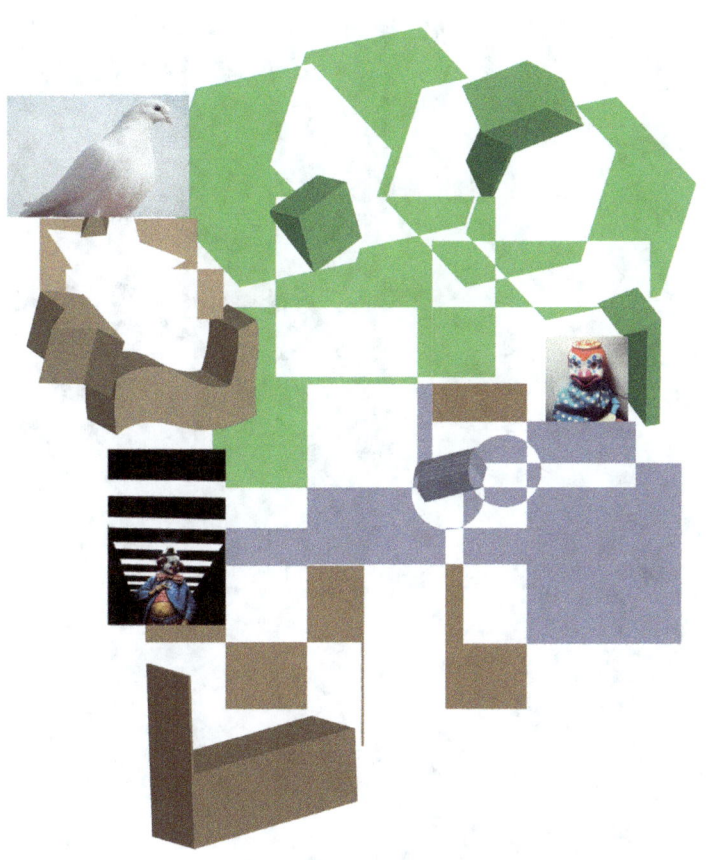

Wild. Adobe Photoshop. 2018.
The world where I live.

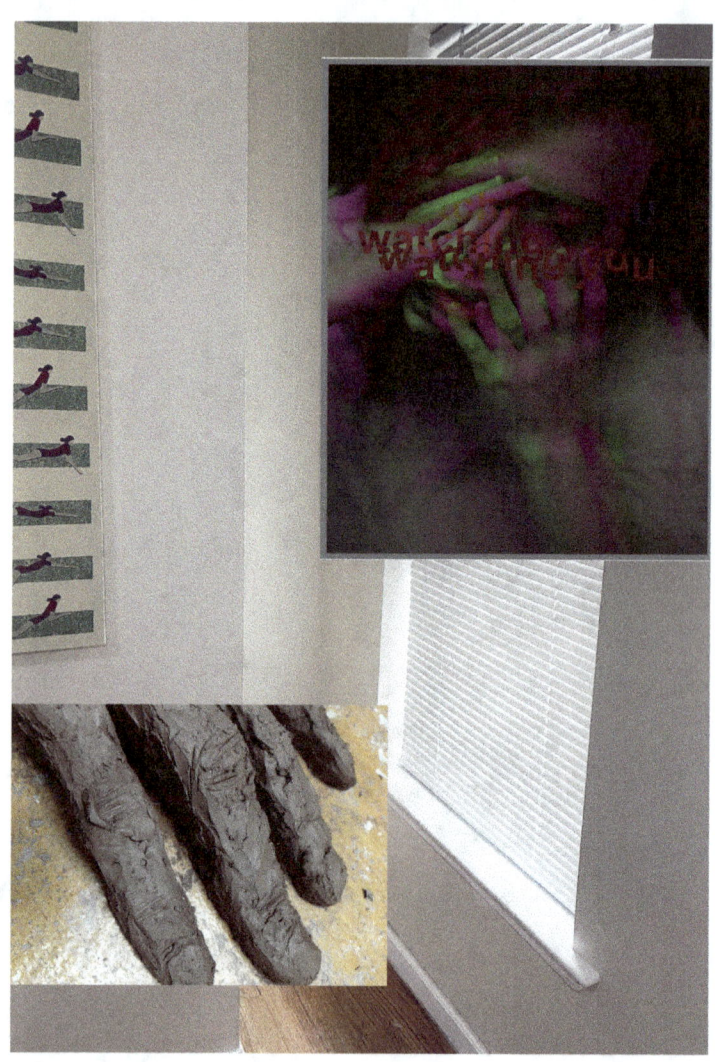

B-16. 2021.

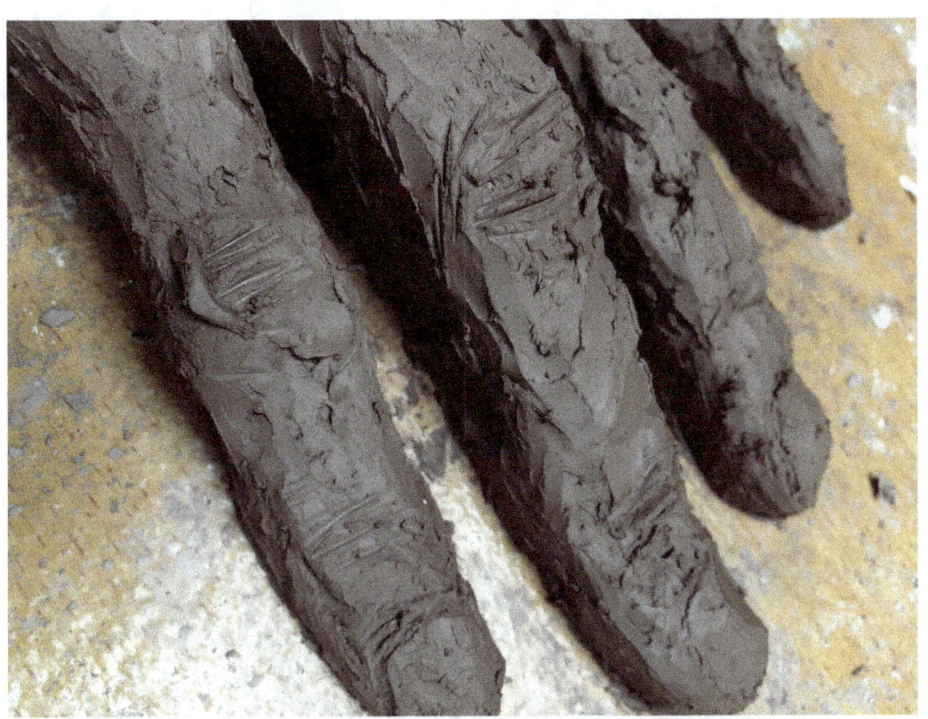

Untitled. Plaster. 2015.
Fingers which have the magic power.
I can do anything with these fingers!

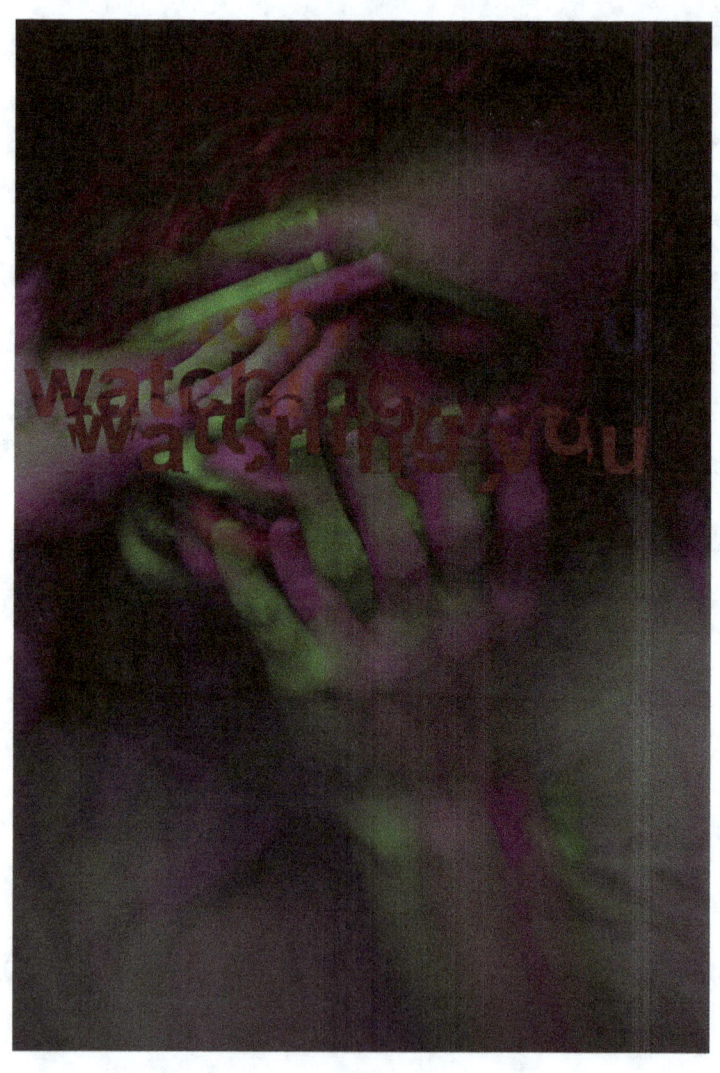

Watching you. Adobe Photoshop. 2019.
You are watching me. Just watching me.

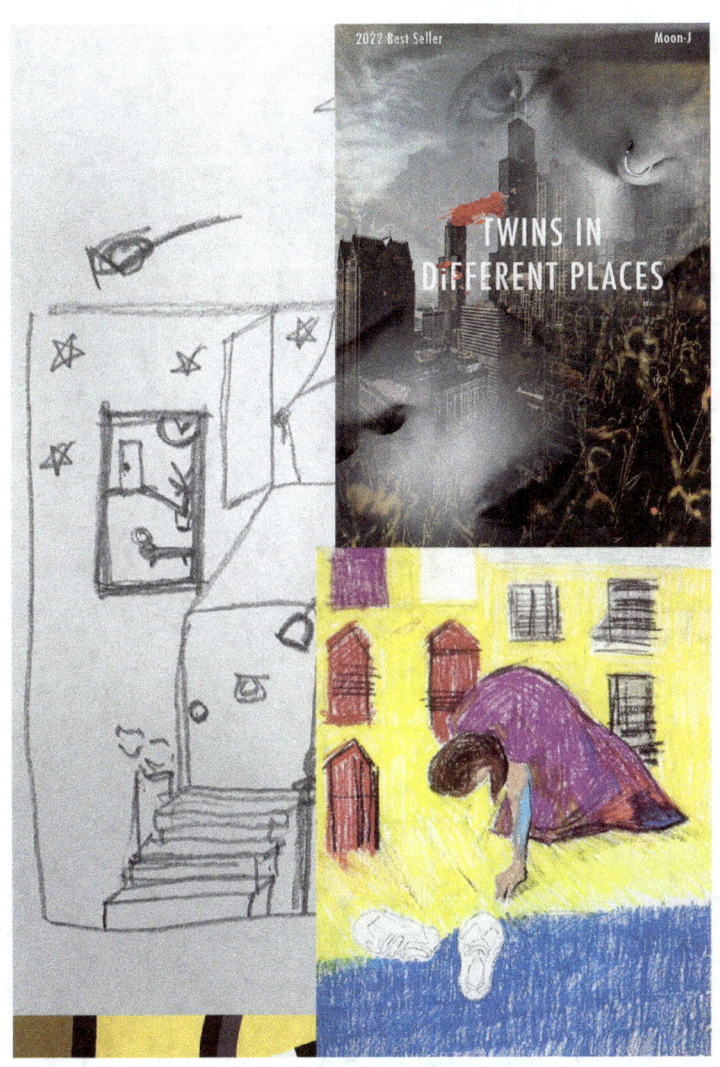

B-17. 2021.

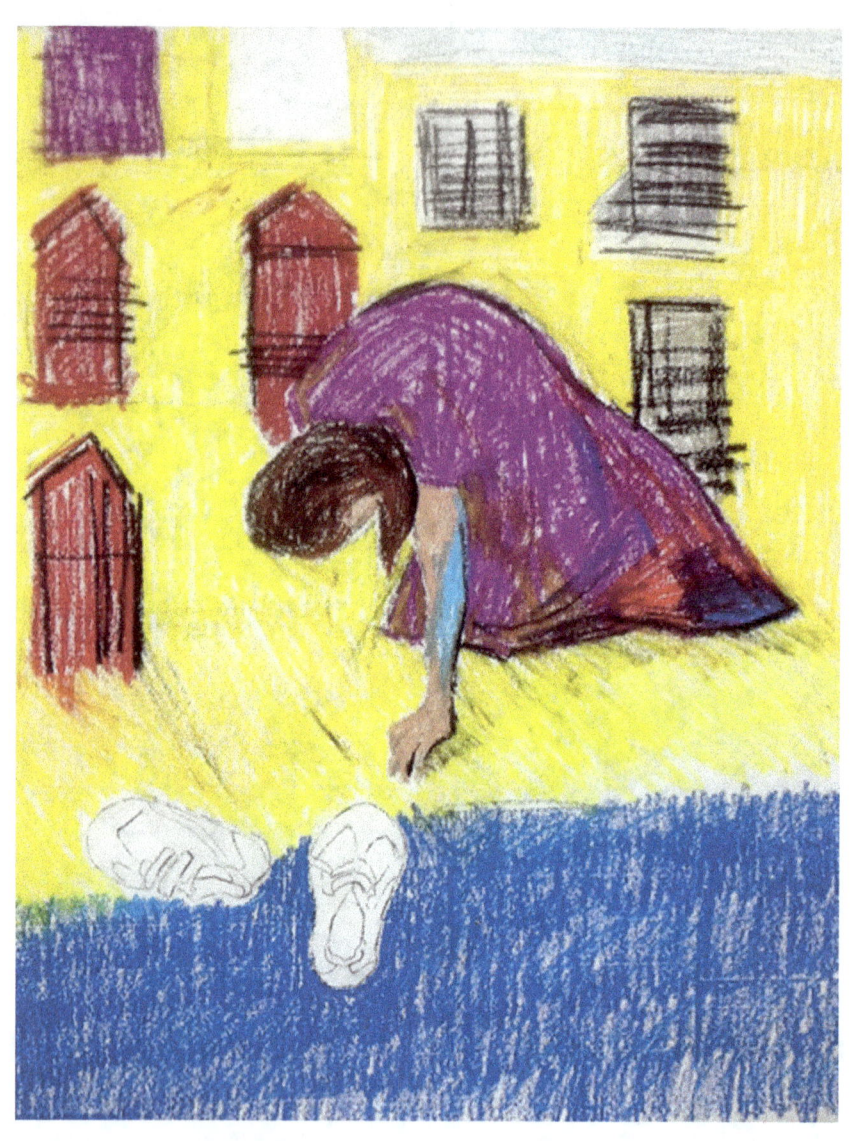

Oh, my child!. Pastel. 2014.
Crying, crying, I'm crying.

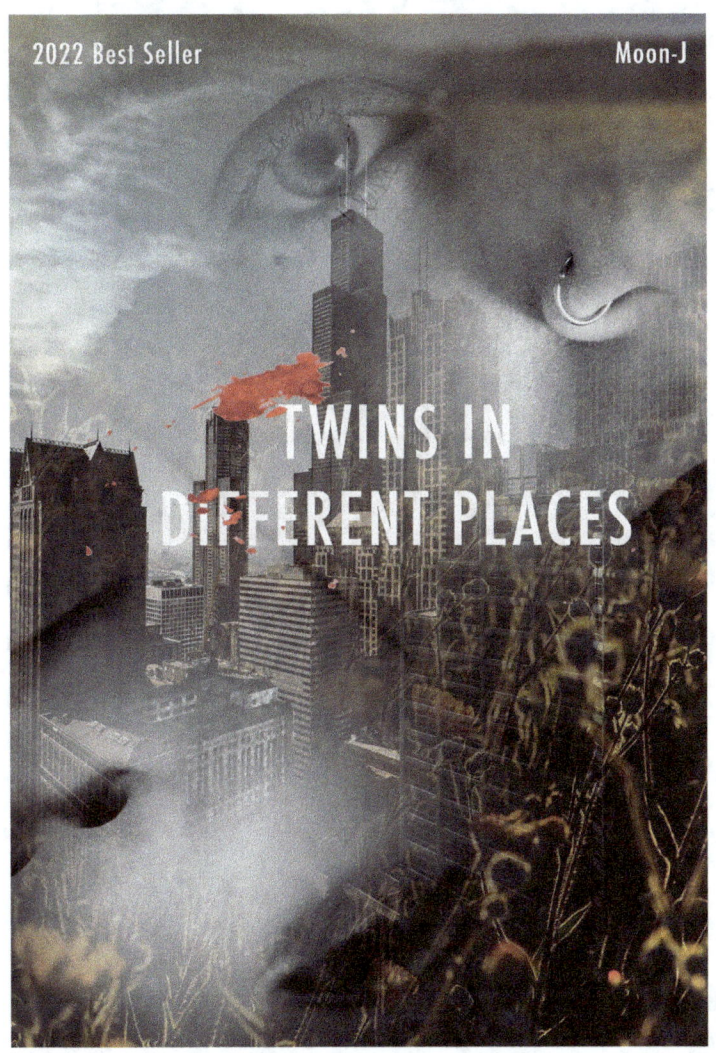

Book Cover design. Adobe Photoshop. 2021.

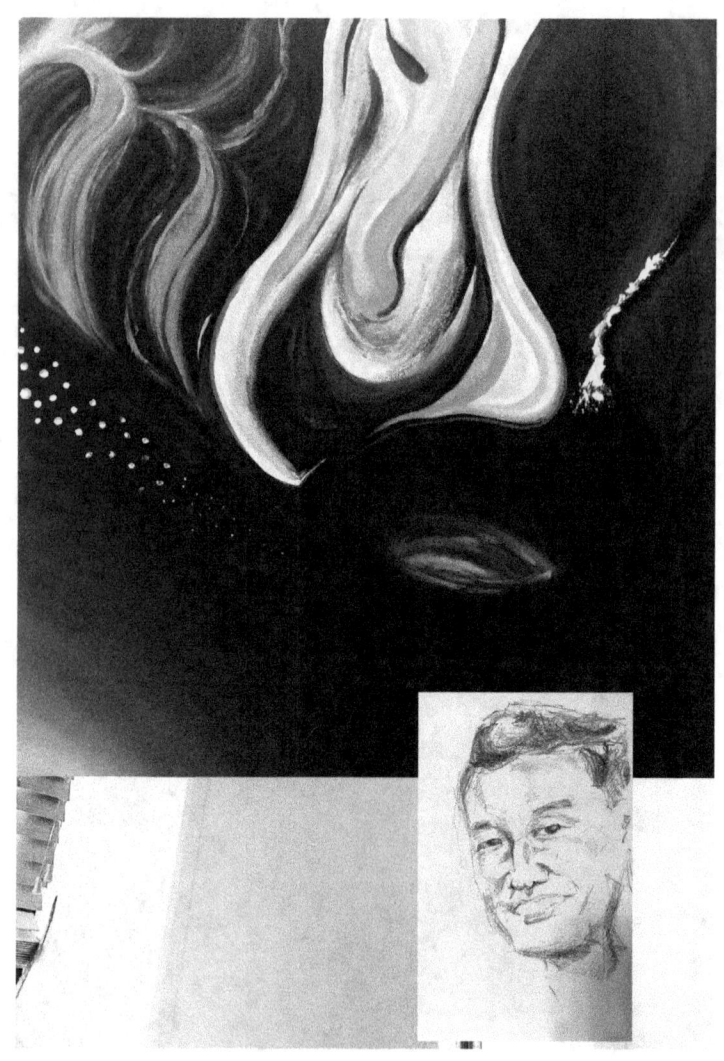

B-18. 2021.

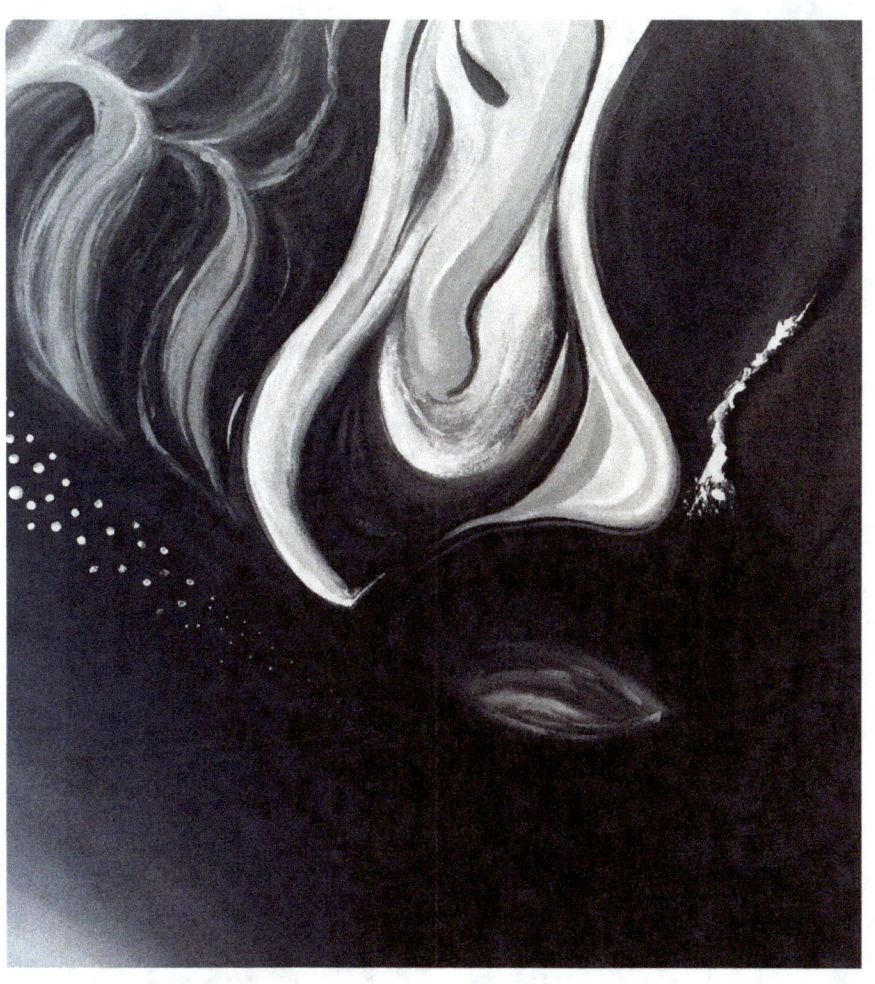

Untitled. Oil. 2015.
Somewhere in that space,
You are waiting for me.

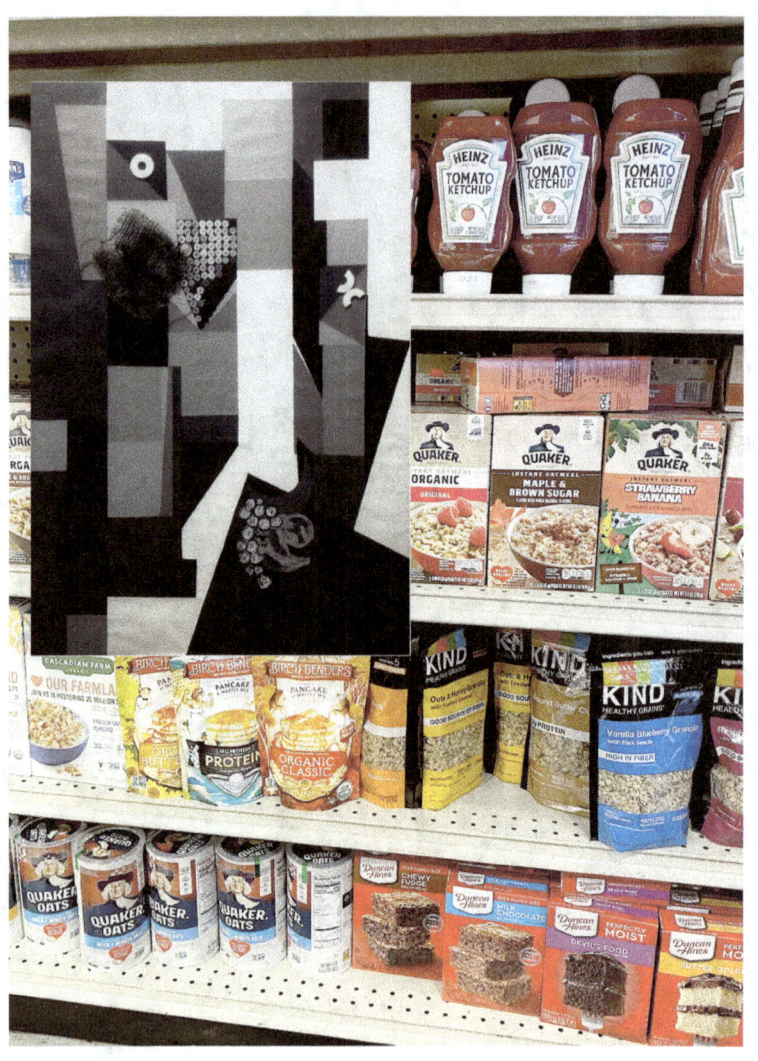

B-19. 2022.

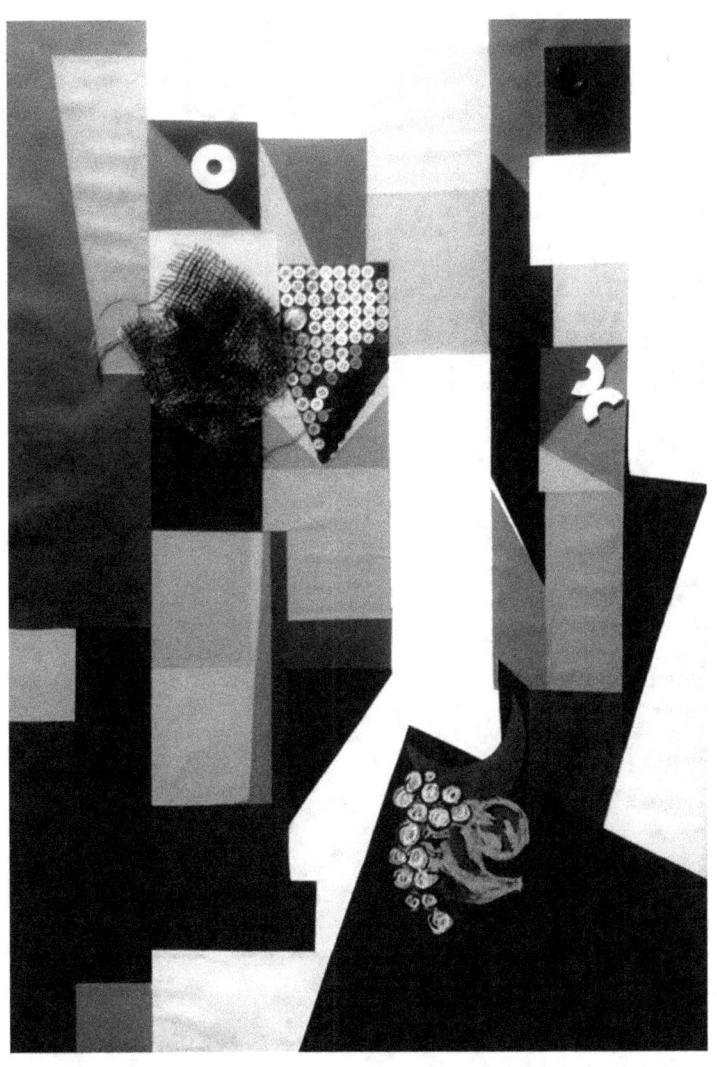

Dedicated to Picaso. Color Papers, Buttons, Charcoal, Fabrics. 2014.

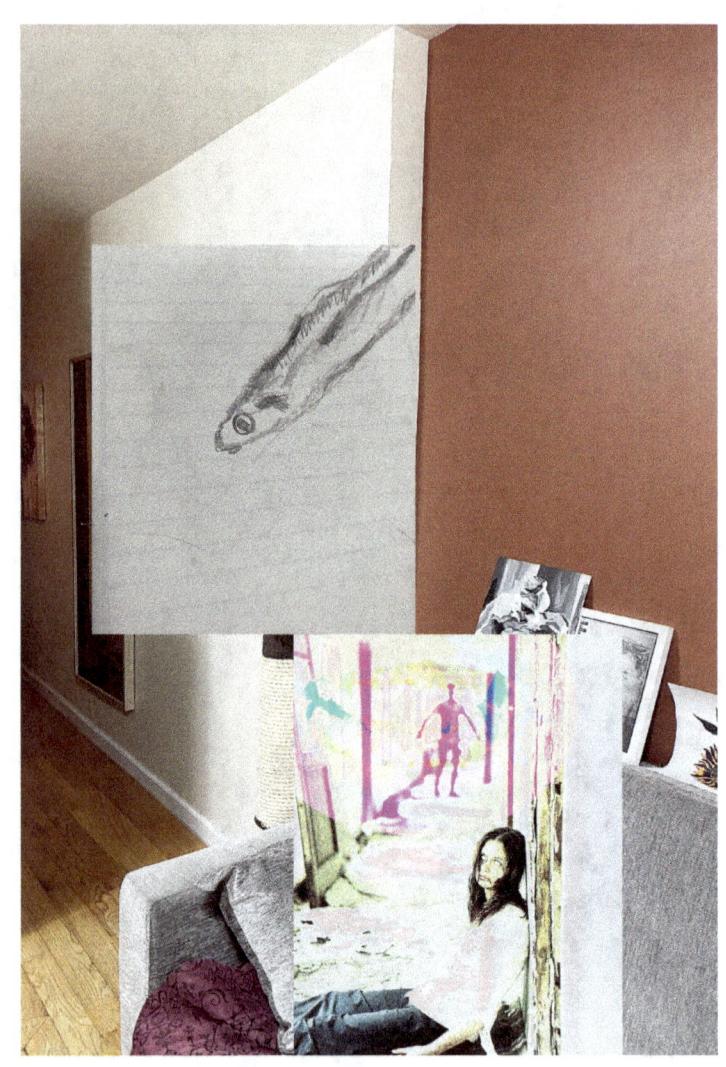

B-20. 2021.

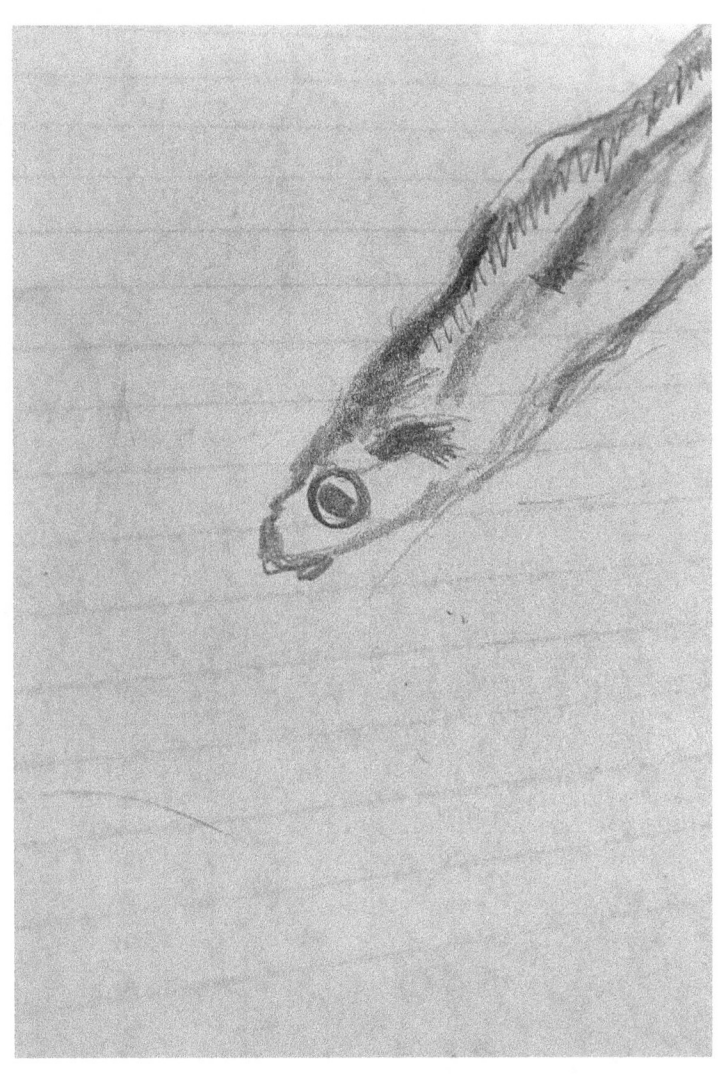

Fish. Pencil. 2010.
Do you wanna draw a fish?

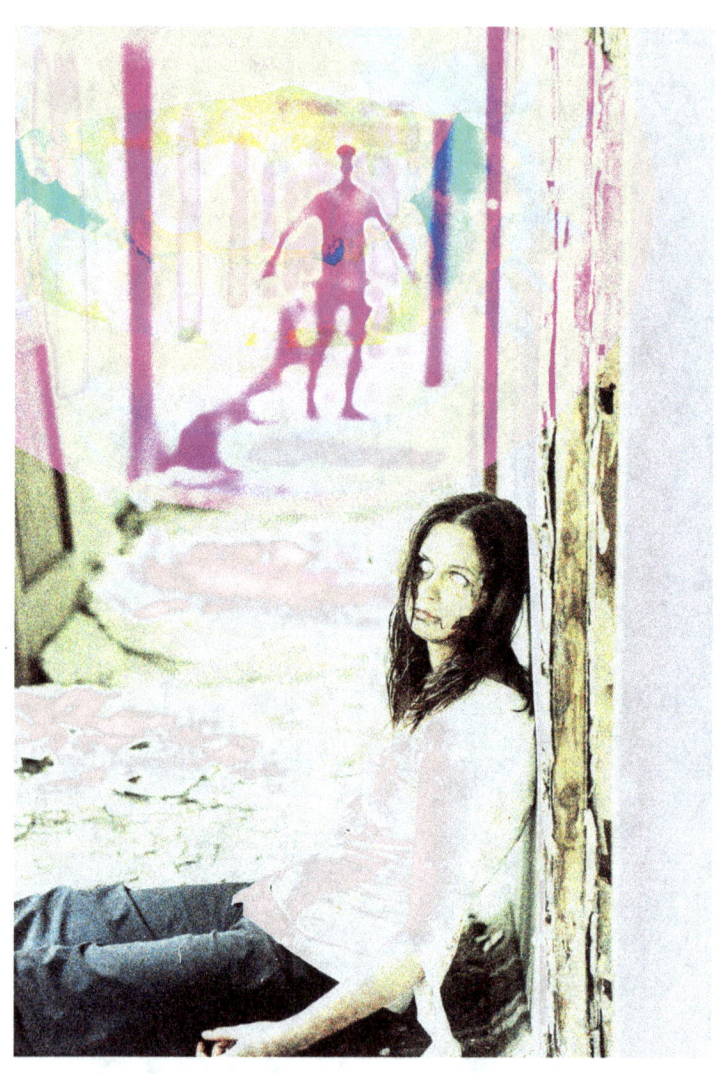

Untitled. Adobe Photoshop. 2019.
Between cognitive and soulless.

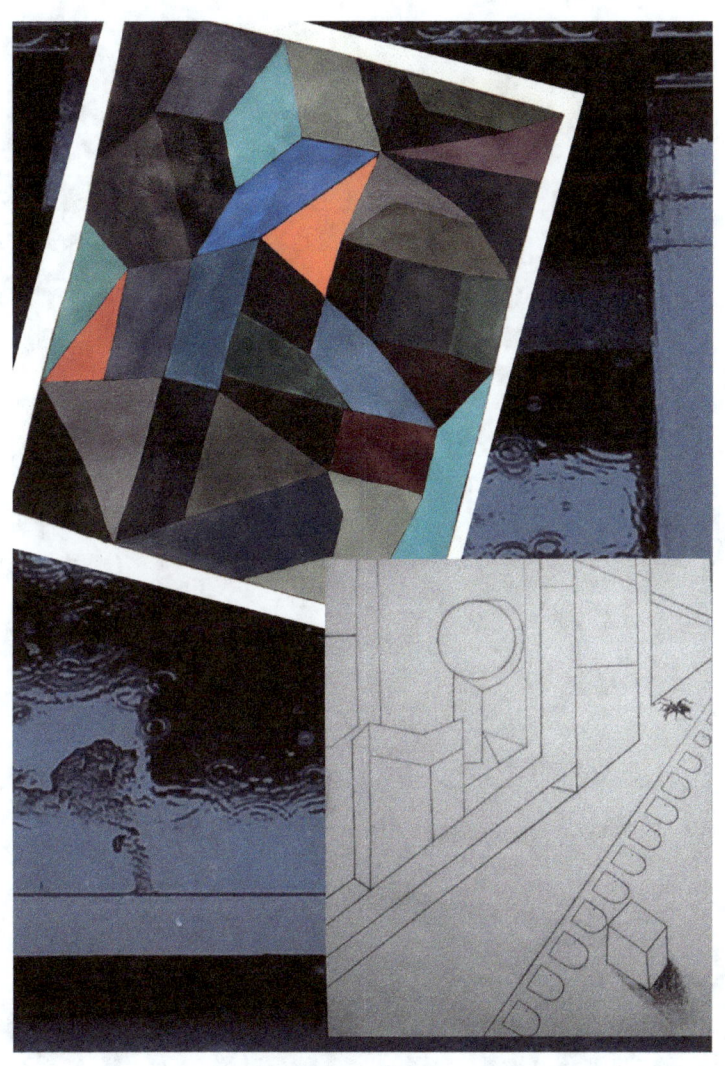

B-21. 2021.

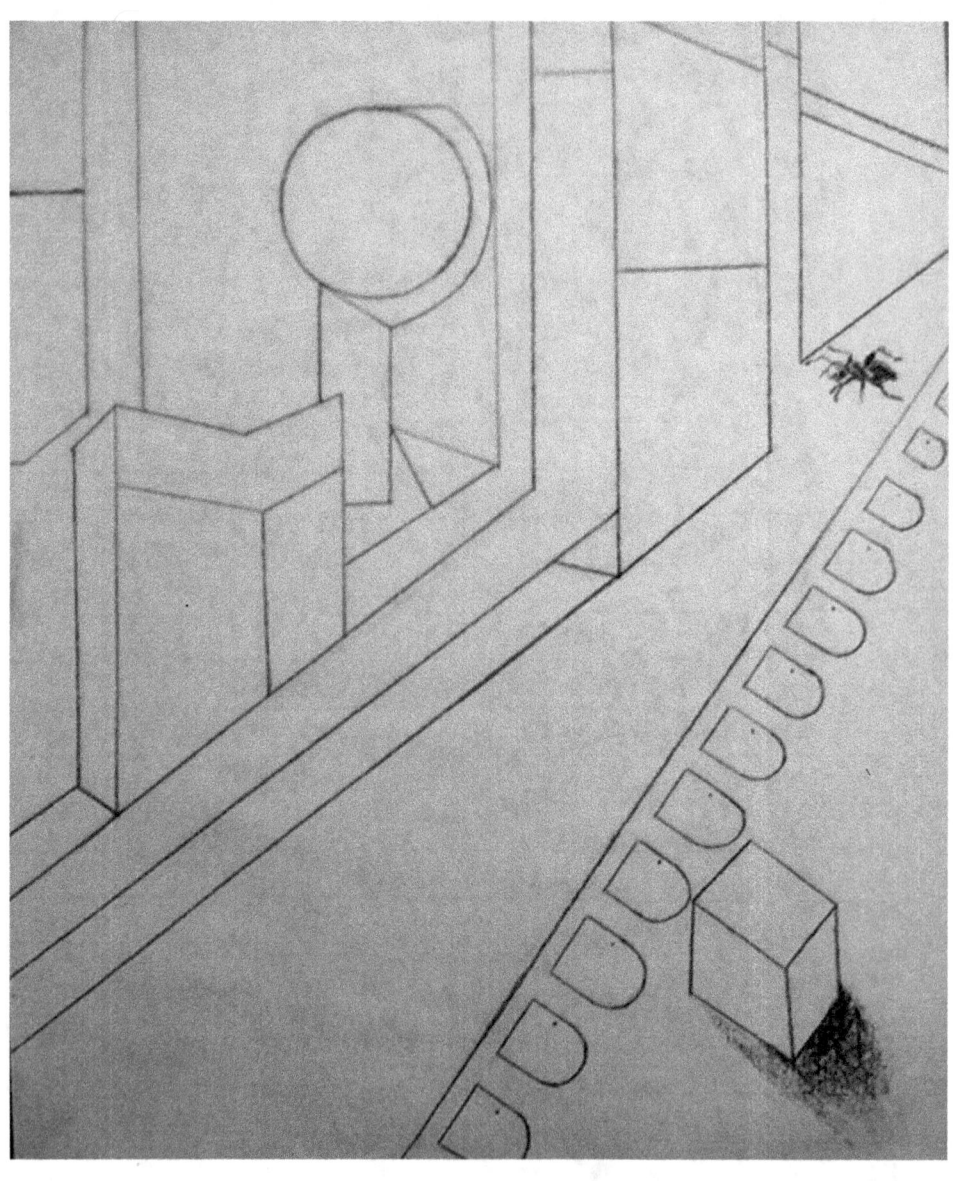

Untitled. Pencil. 2015.

Me in this world.

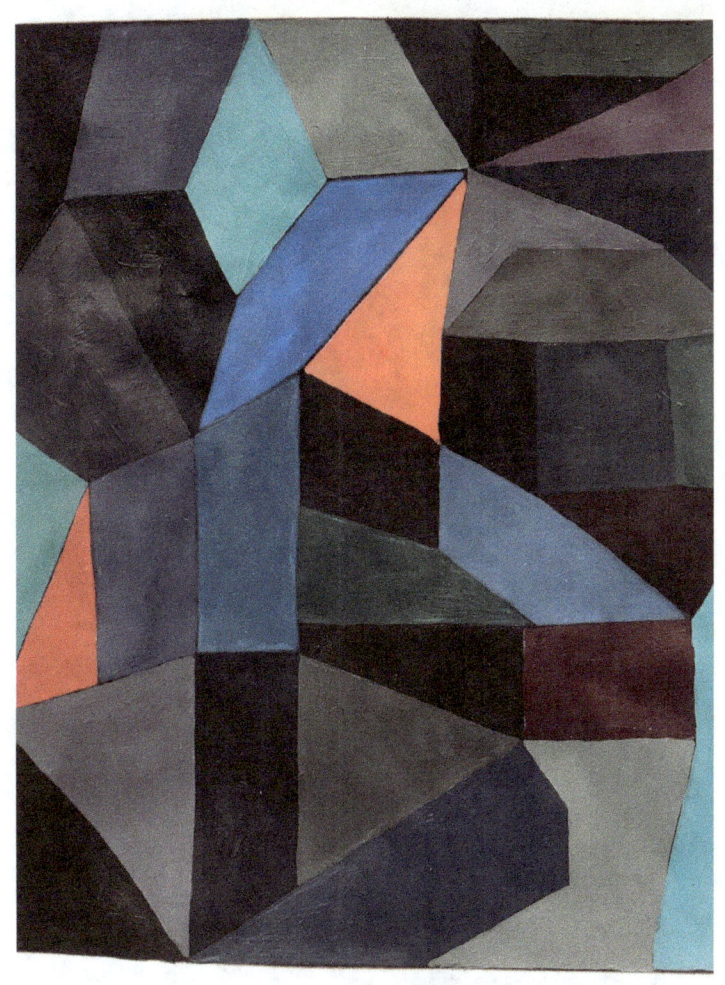

Color block. Acrylic. 2016.

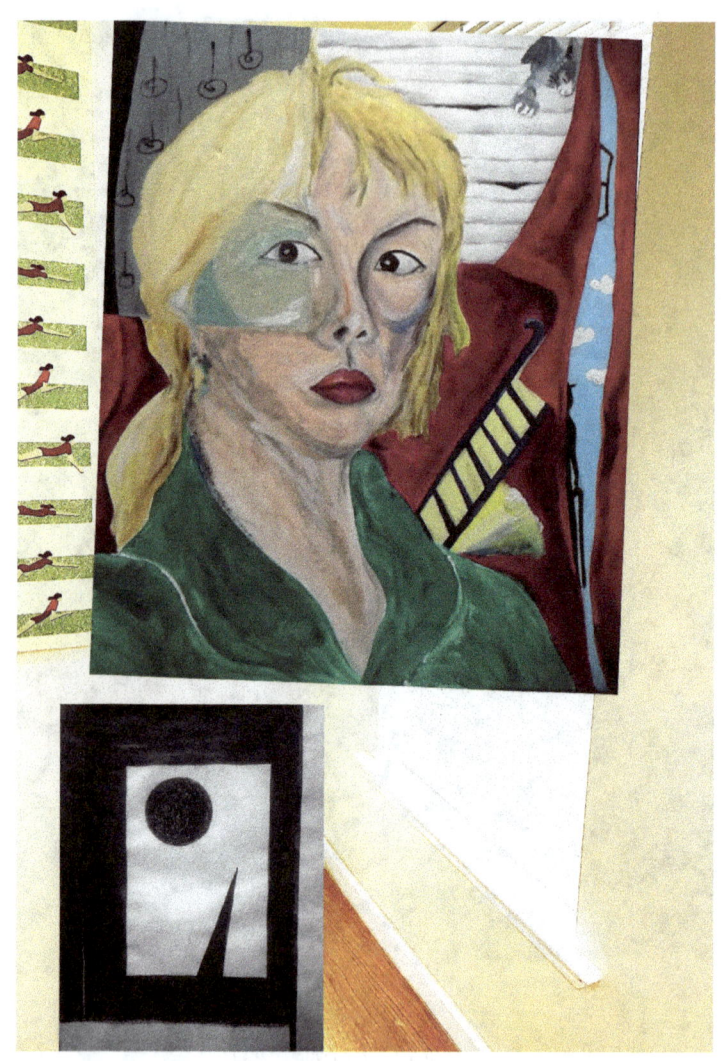

B-22. 2021.

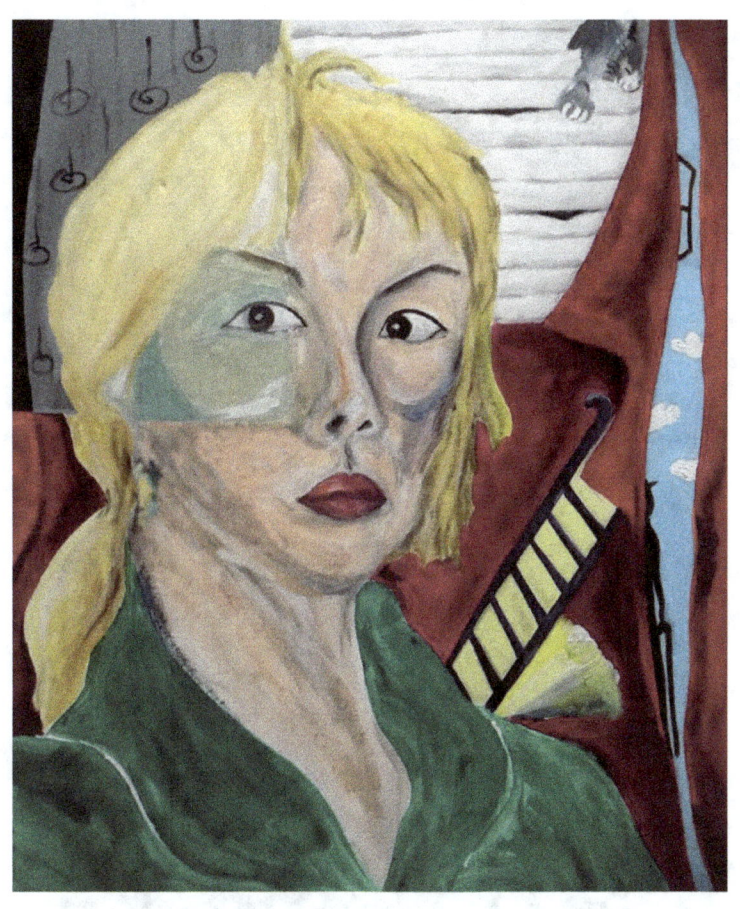

Untitled. Acrylic. 2016.
I dream about so many stories. Sometimes, I see tomorrow.

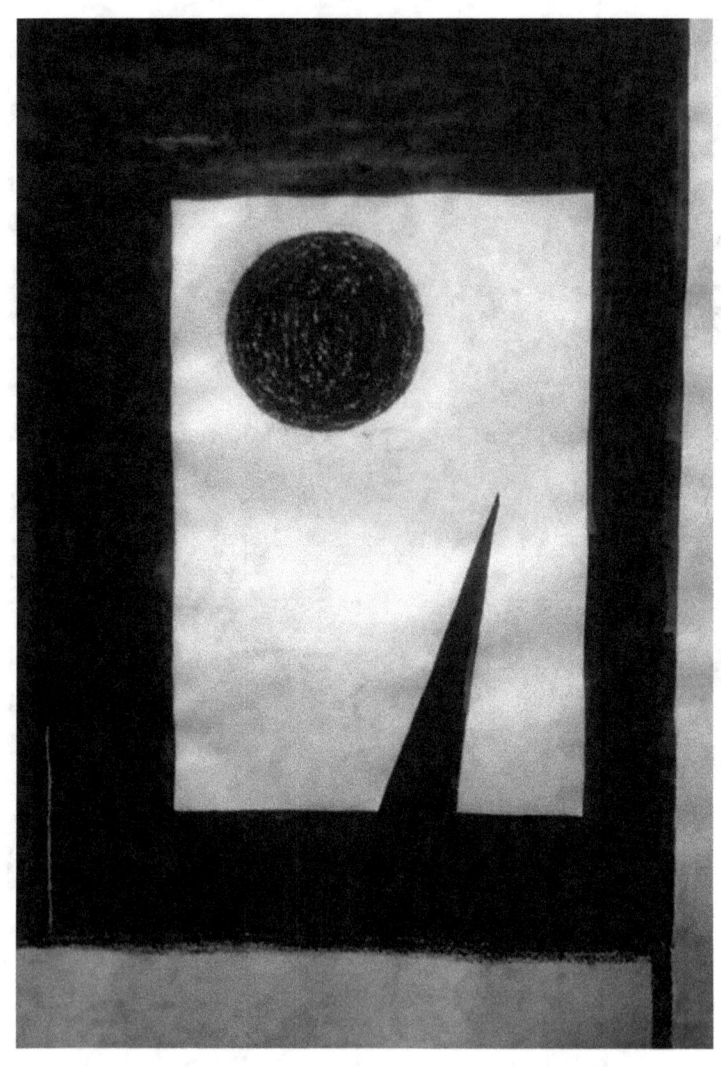
Untitled. Ink & Charcoal. 2015.

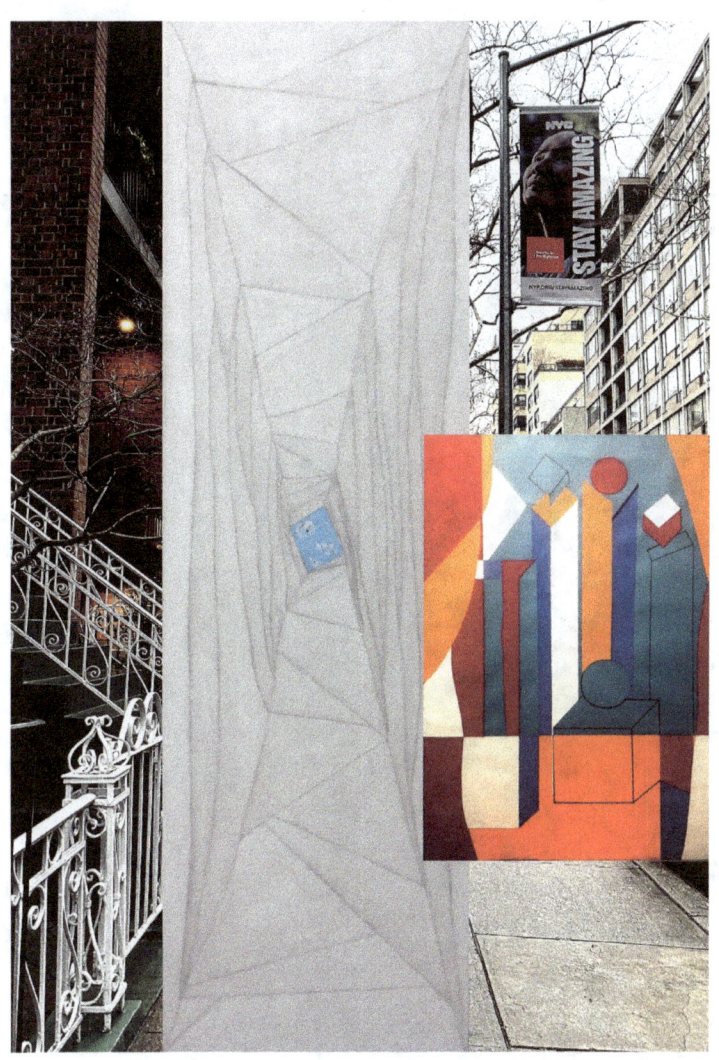

B-23. 2022

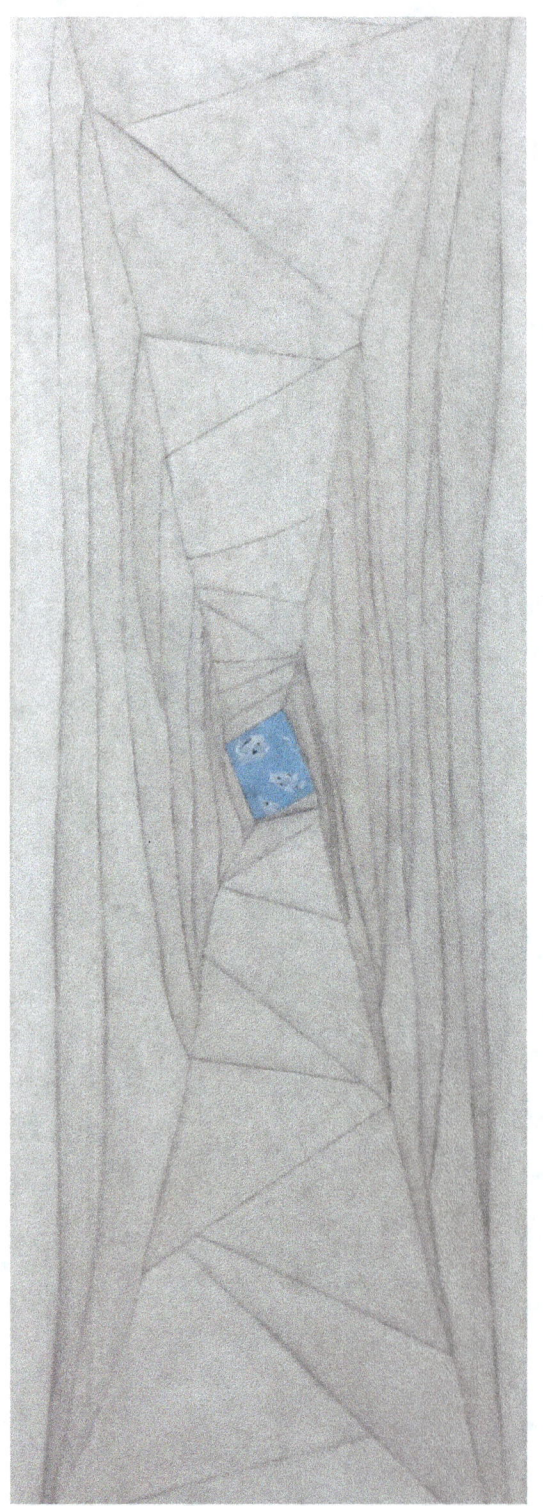

The well. Acrylic.
2014.

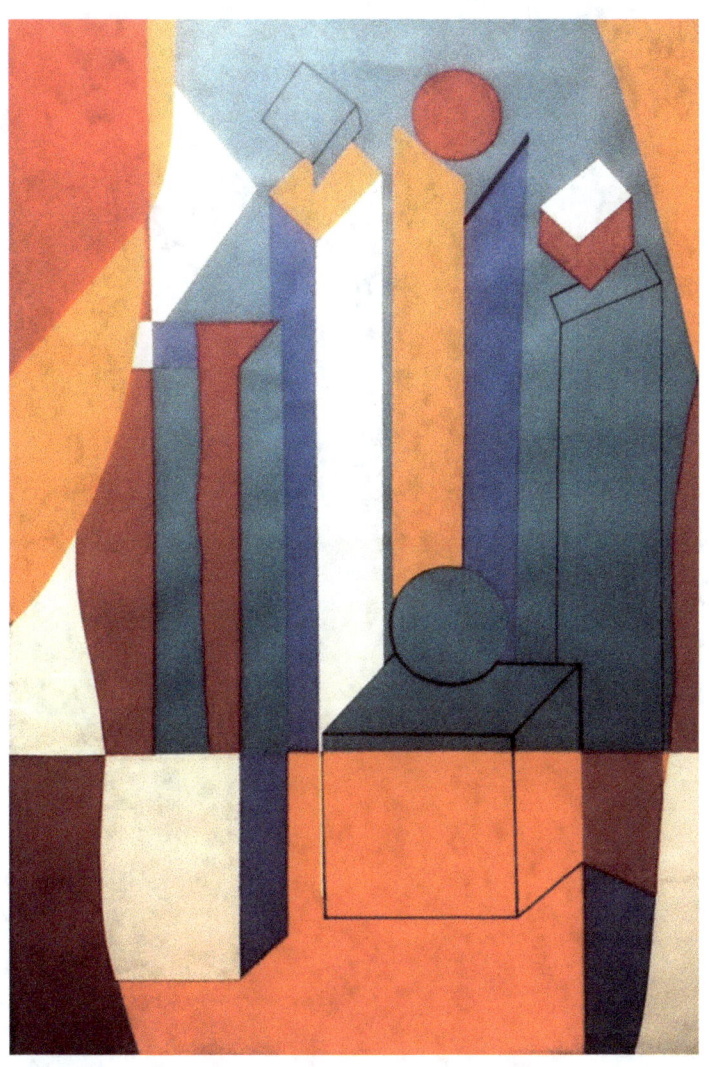
A group of people. Color Paper & Pen. 2014.
They were behind the curtain.

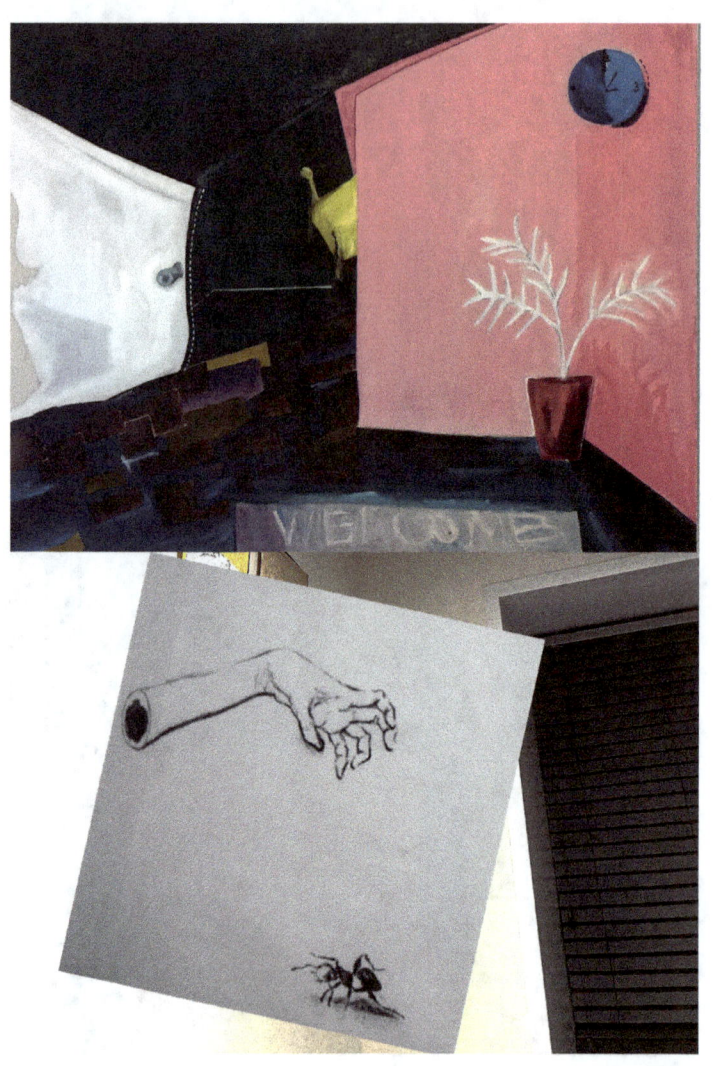

B-24. 2021.

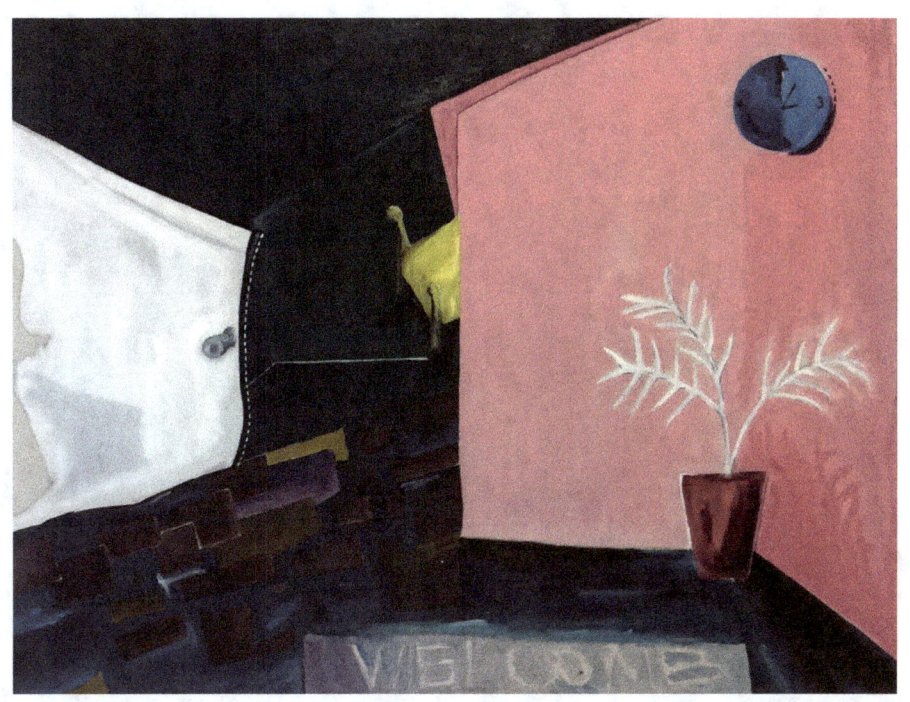

My home. Acrylic. 2015.

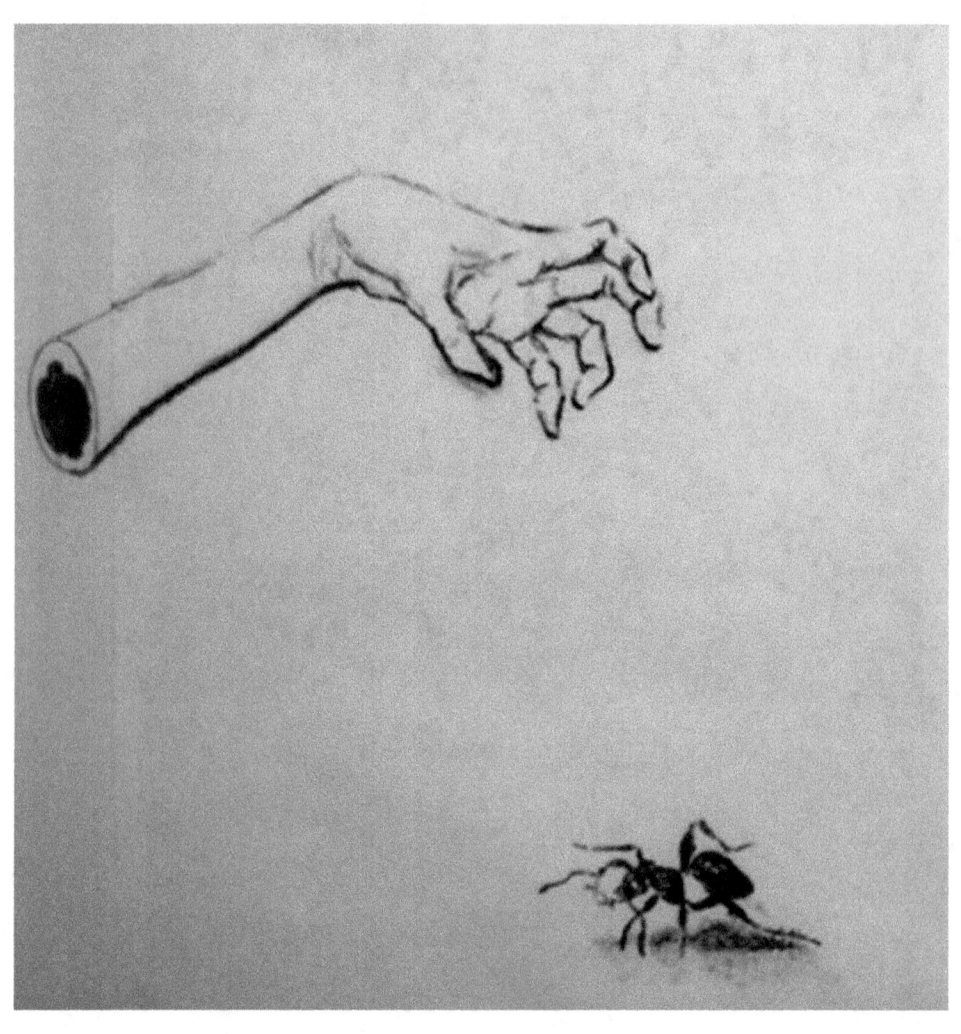

Capitalism. Charcoal. 2015.
You are killing me. I'm broken!

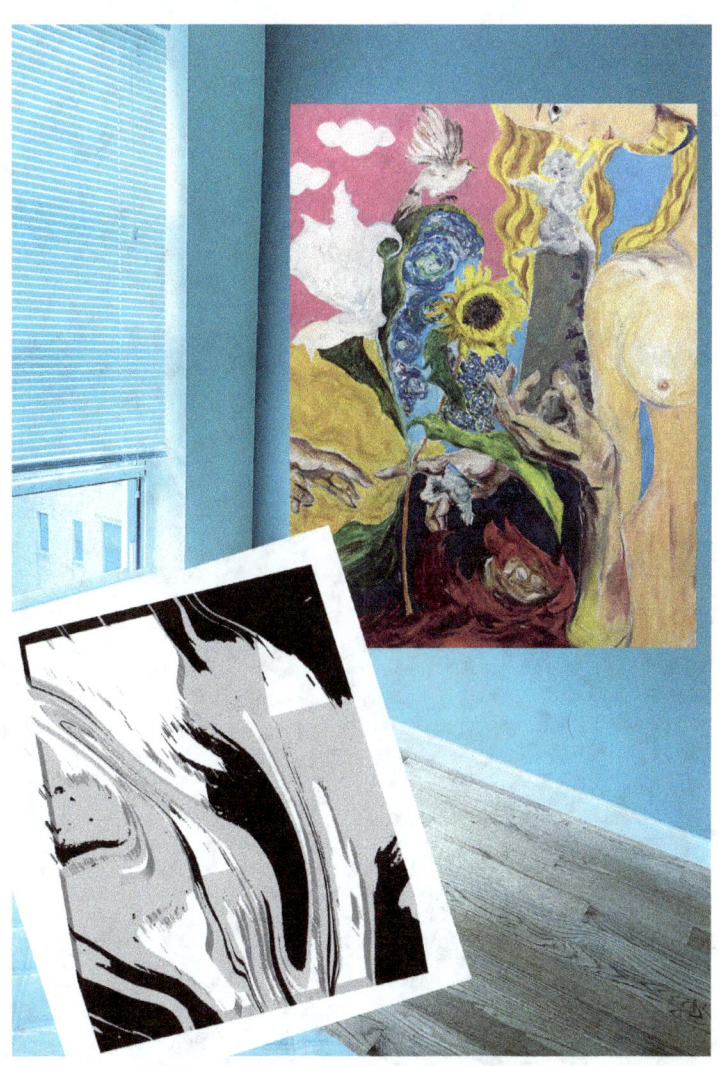

B-25. 2021.

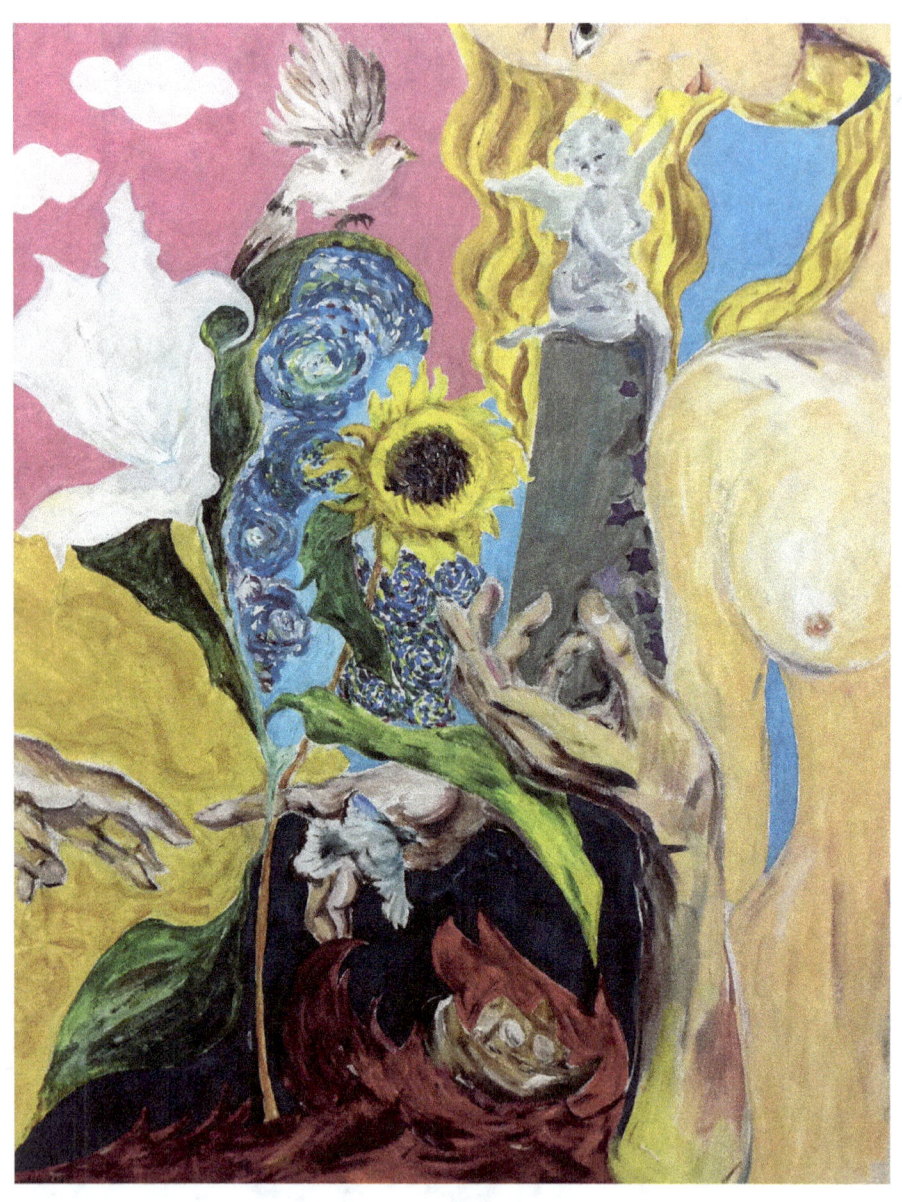

Myth. Acrylic. 2014.
If I have just one more chance to go back,

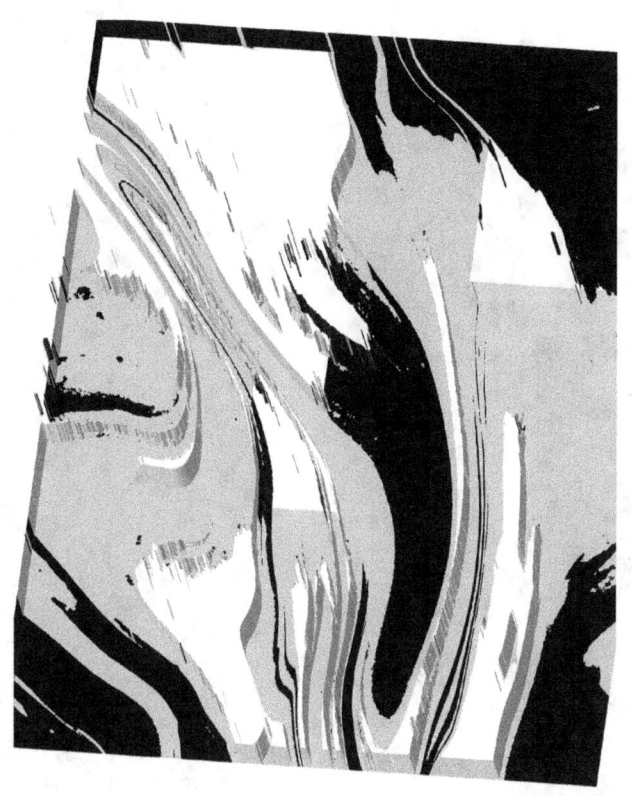

Untitled. Adobe Photoshop. 2018.

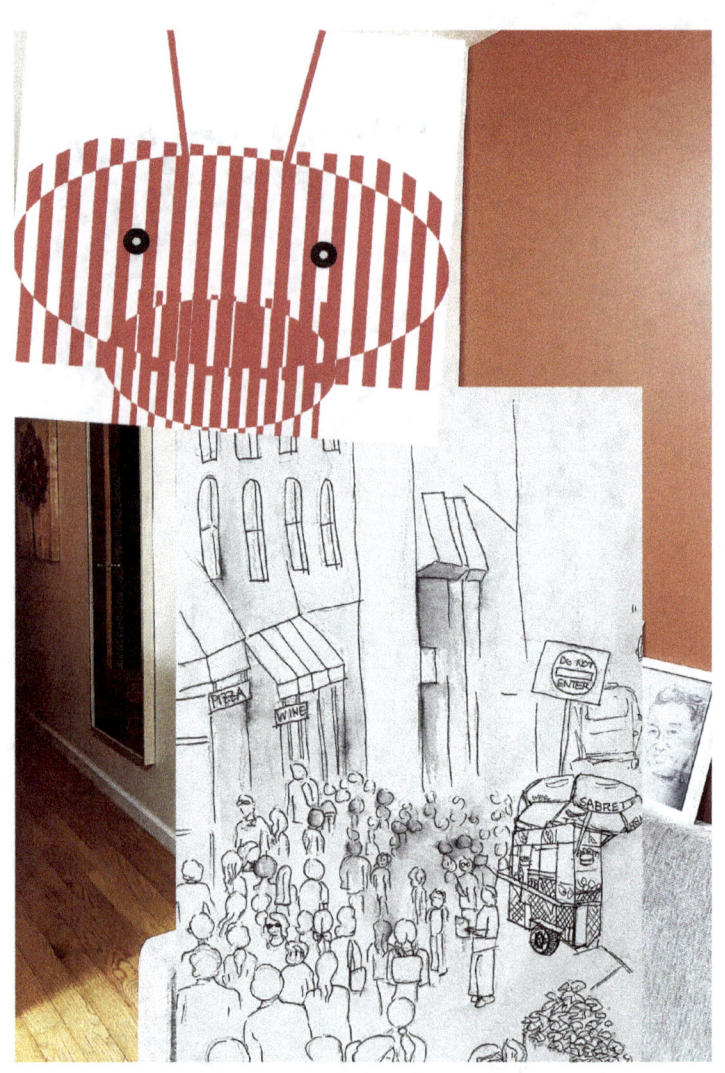

B-26. 2021.

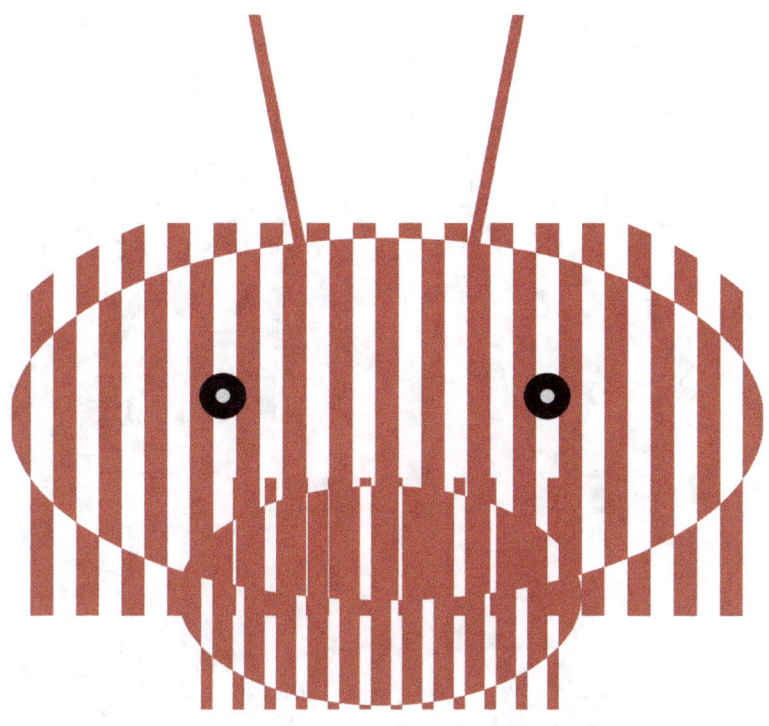

Grasshopper. Adobe Illustrator. 2020.

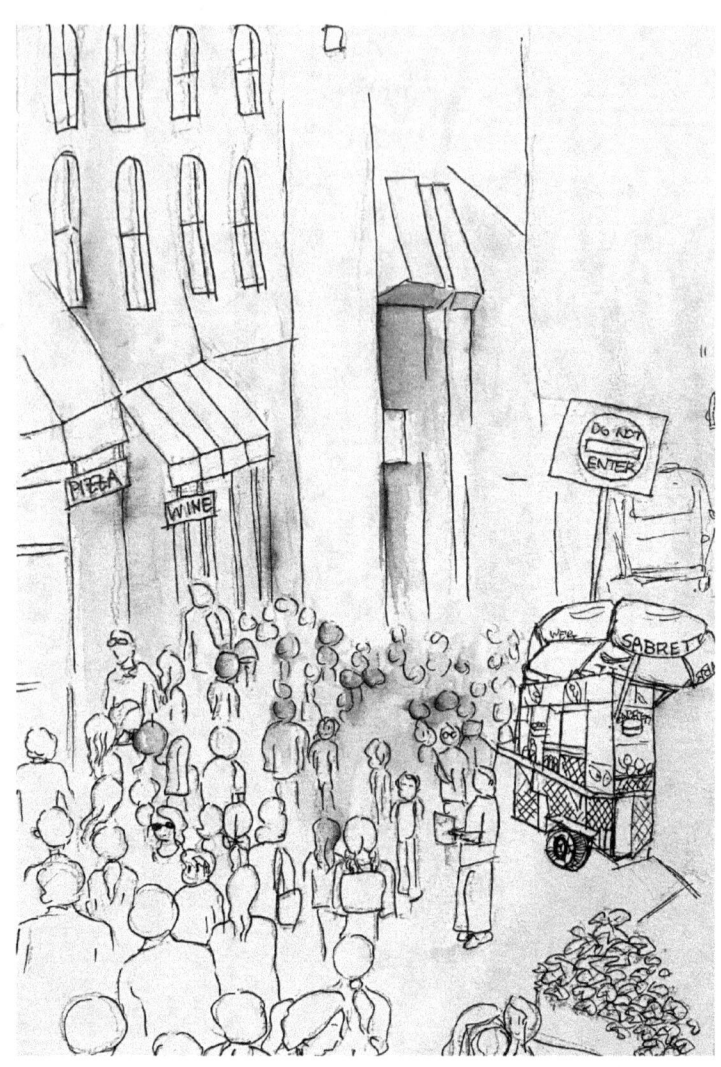

The Street. Pen. 2020.

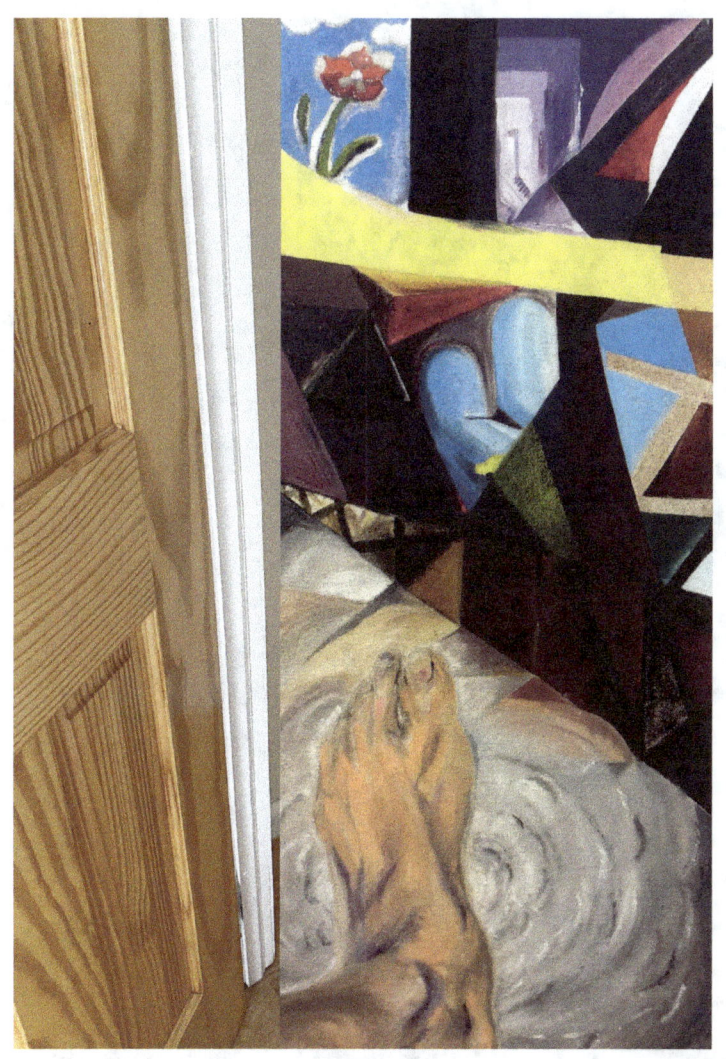

B-27. 2022.

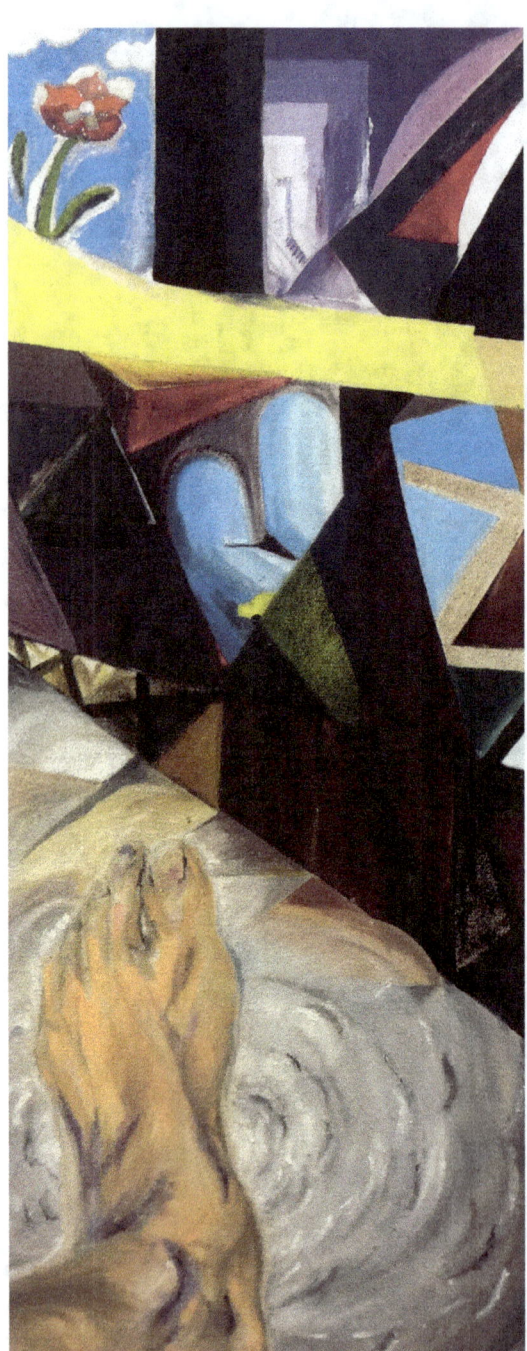

Untitled. Oil. 2015.
I stepped on the city.

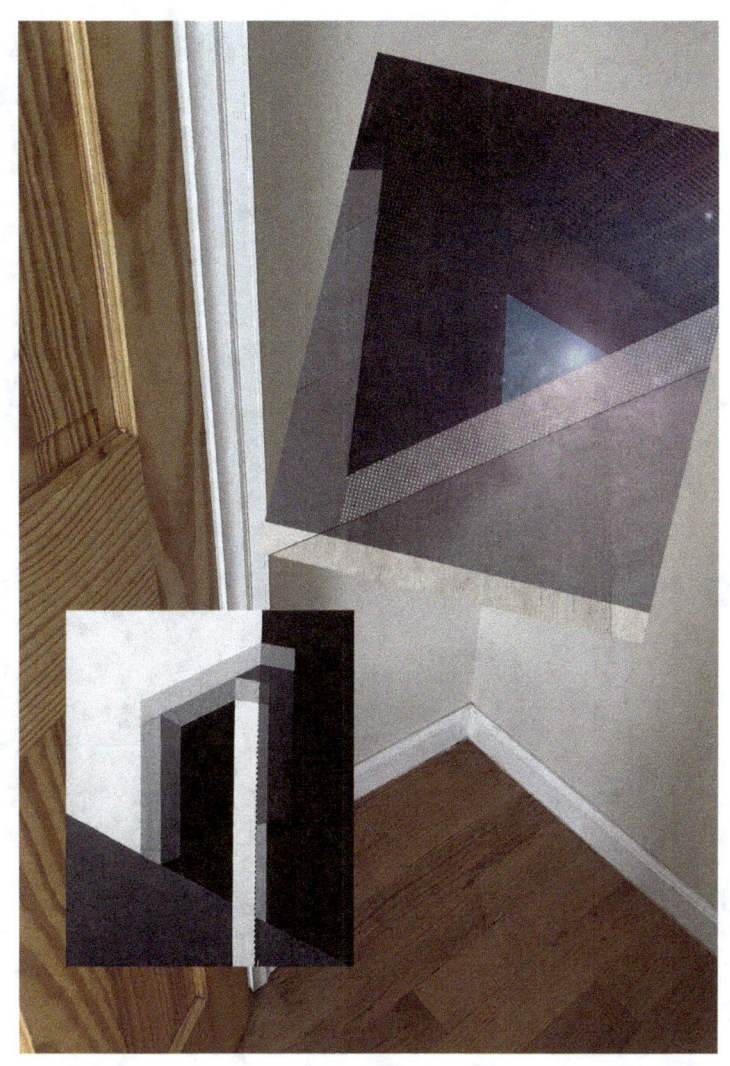

B-28. 2021.

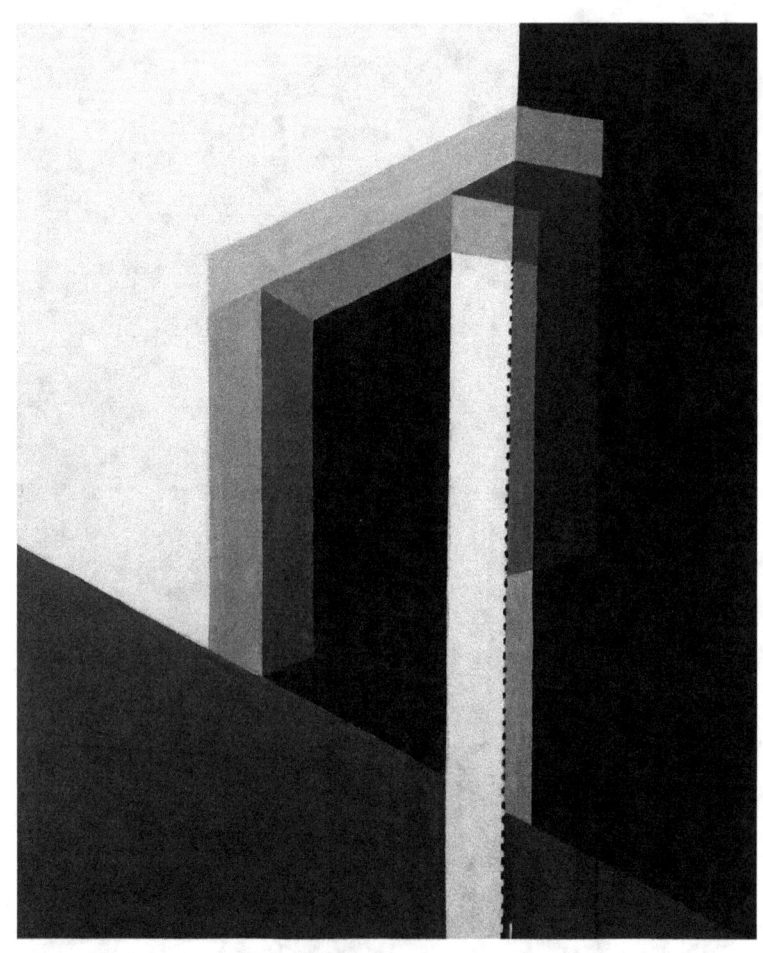

A Door. Acrylic. 2014.
   Open the door and let me in, please. P.

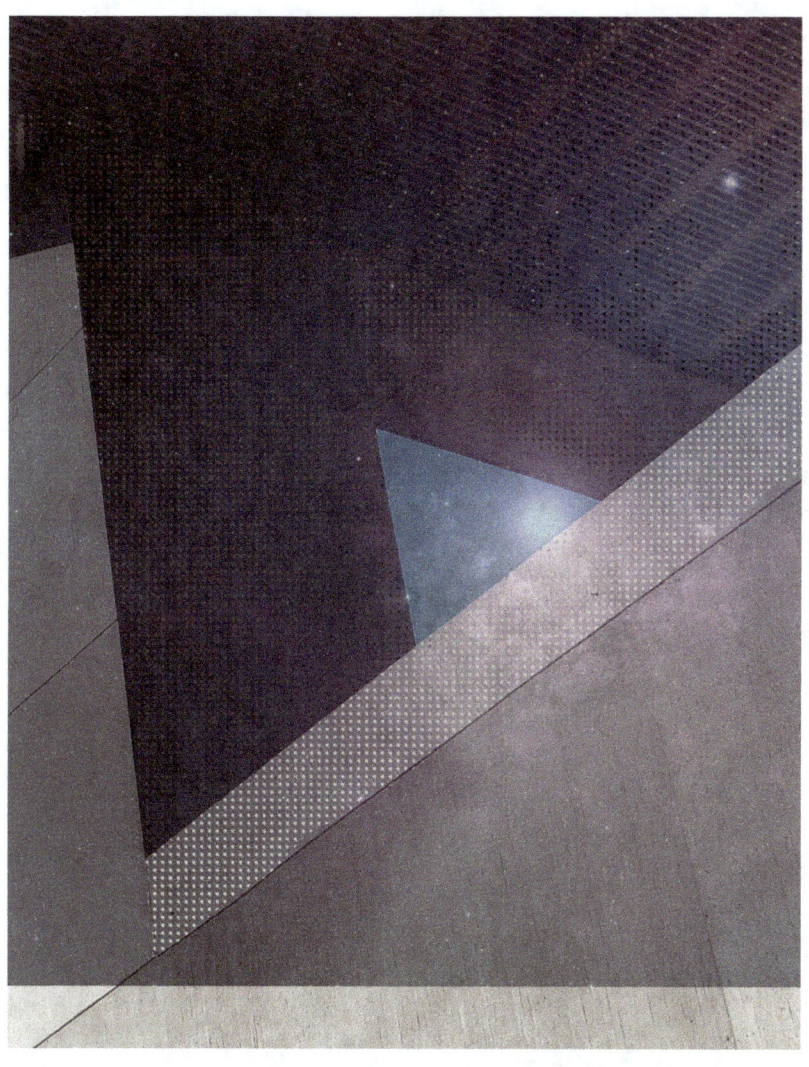

Moonlight. Adobe Photoshop. 2019.
I can see you when I close my eyes. One summer day.

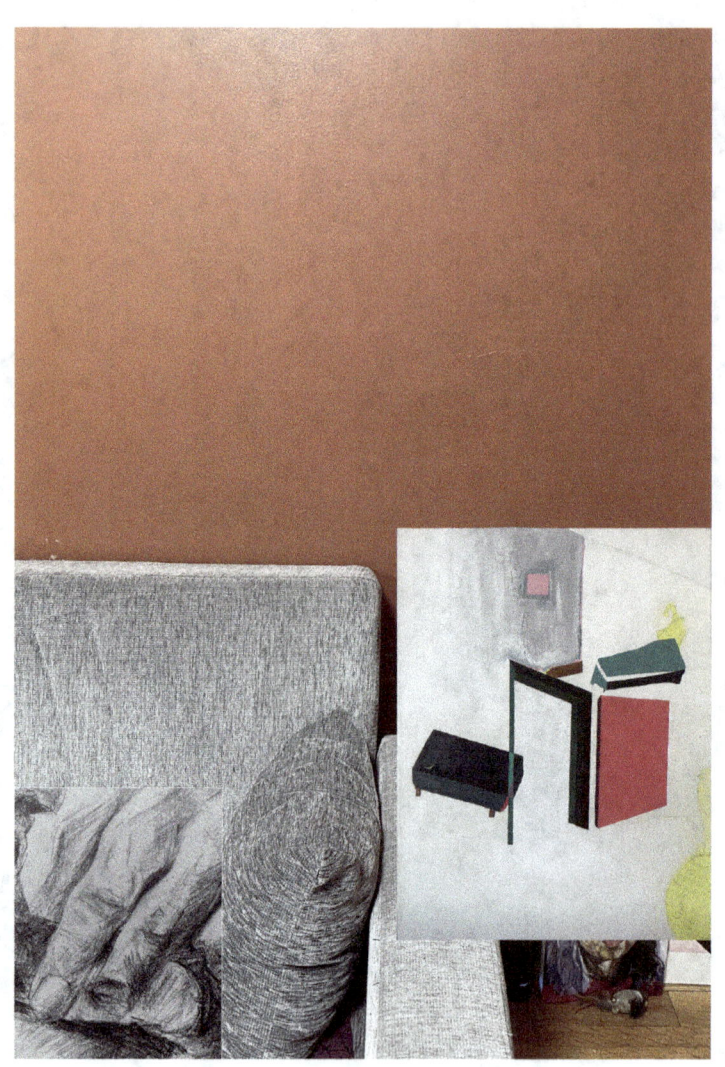

B-29. 2021.

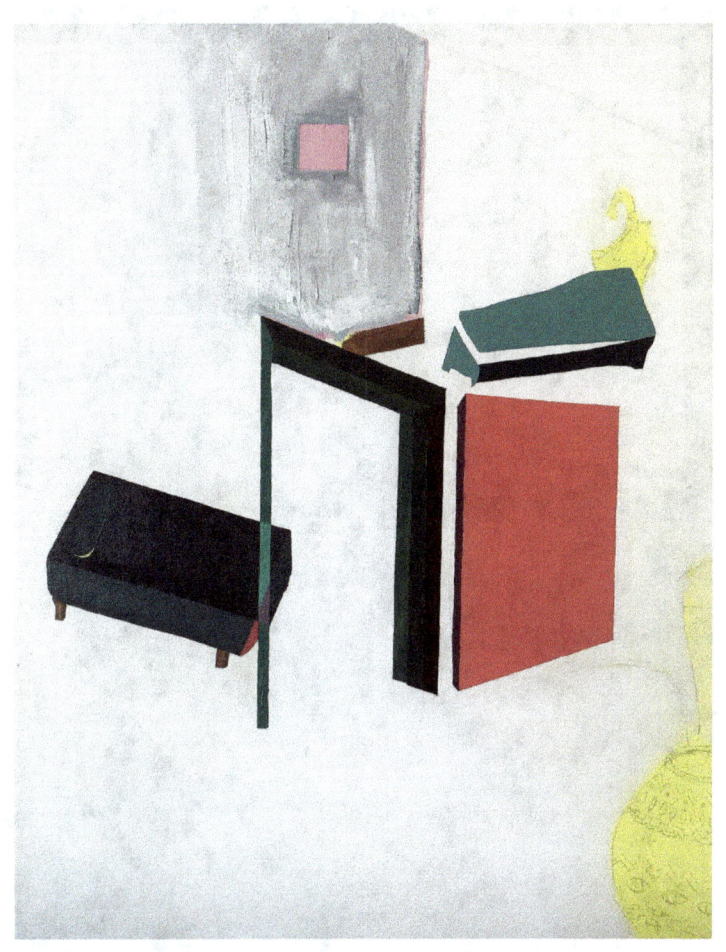

A Room. Oil. 2017.

Unfinished.

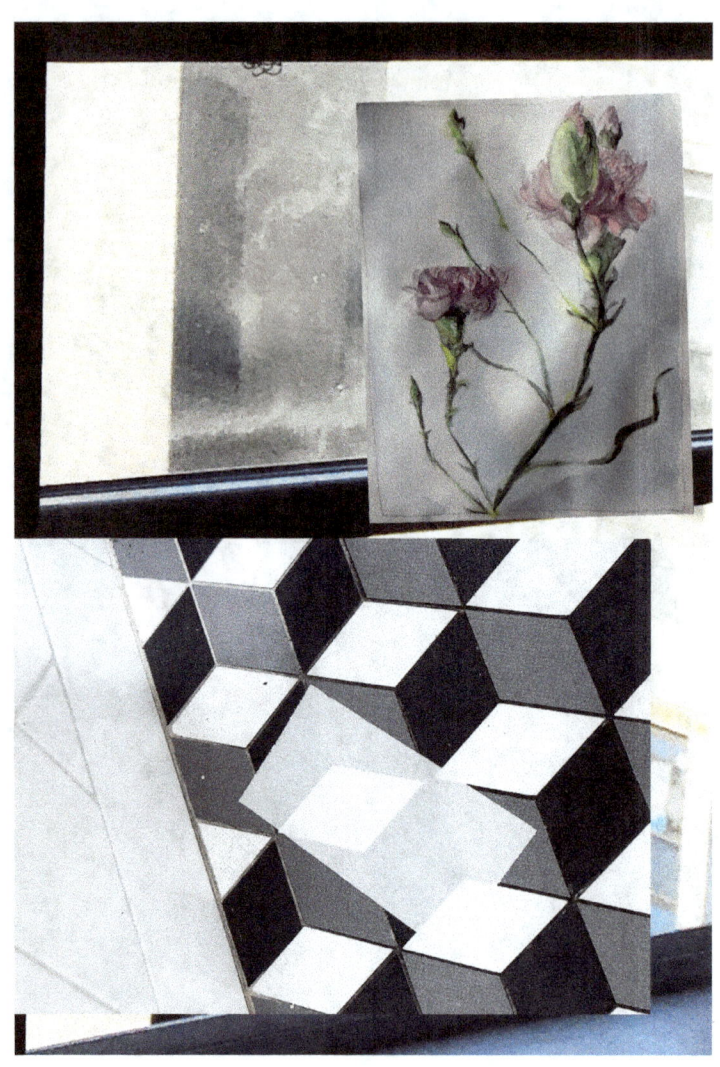

B-30. 2021.

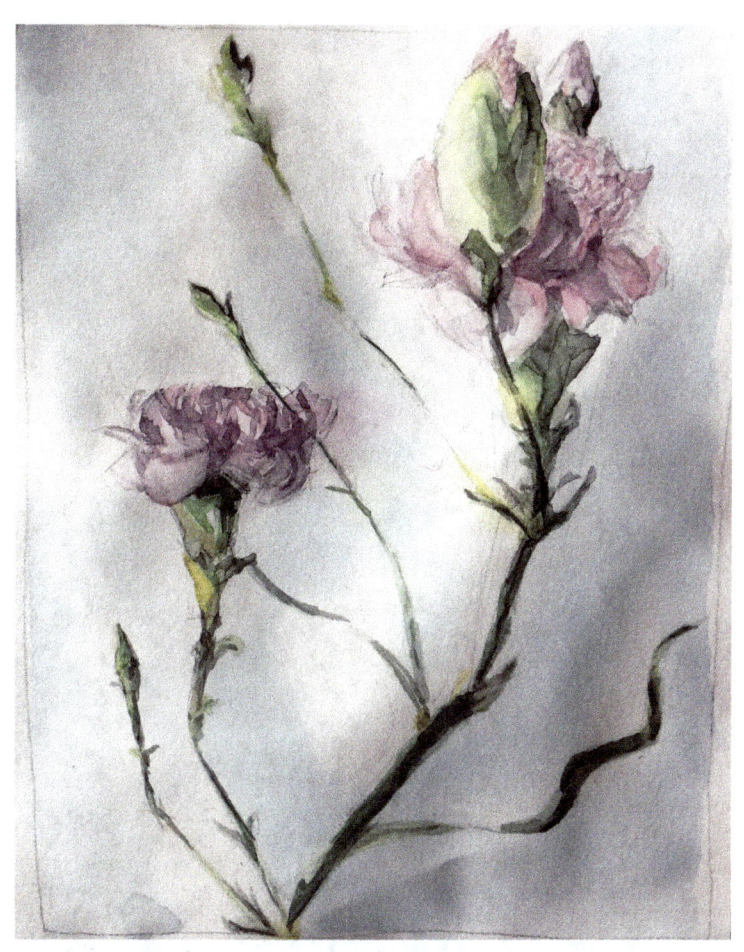

Roses. Watercolor. 2016.
When I move in, you will visit me with flowers.

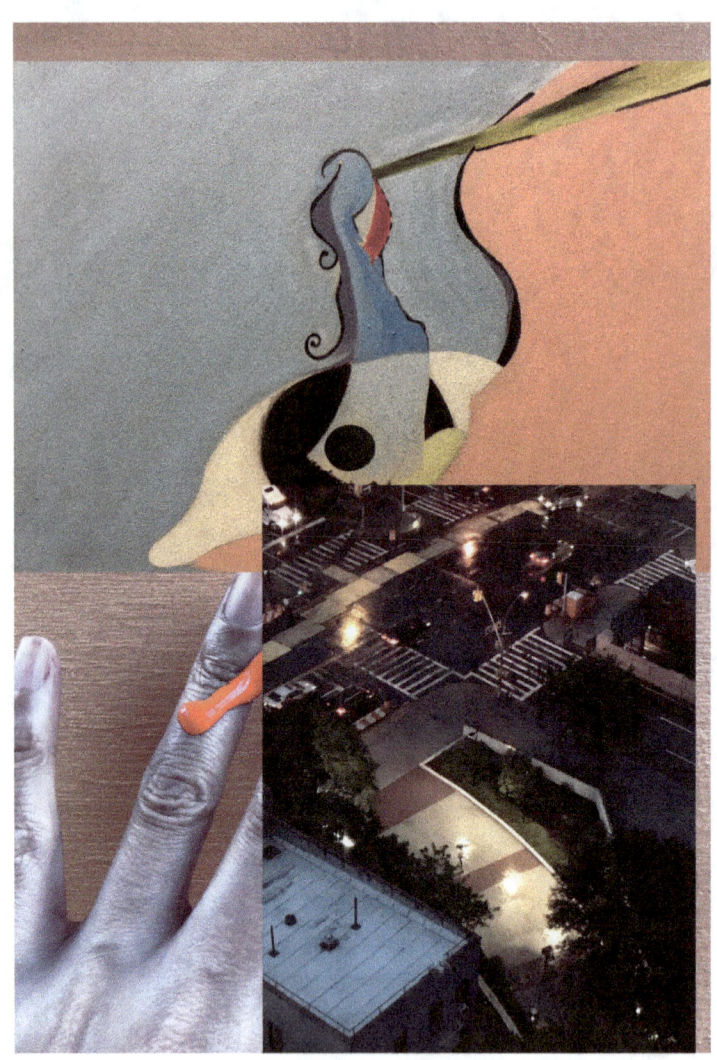

B-31. 2022

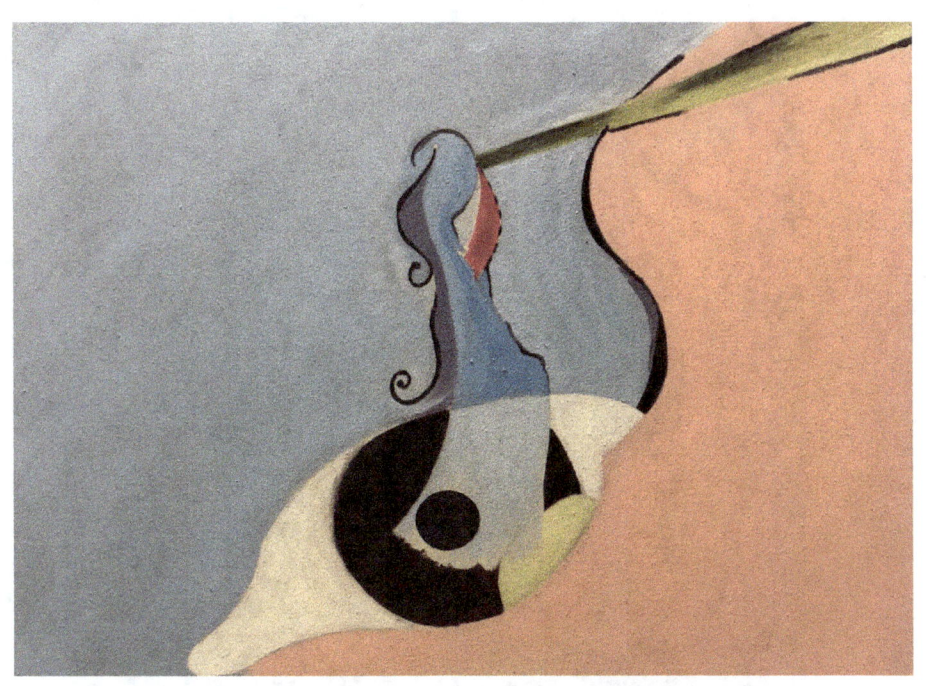

Teardrops. Acrylic. 2016.
I'm crying over you, over you.

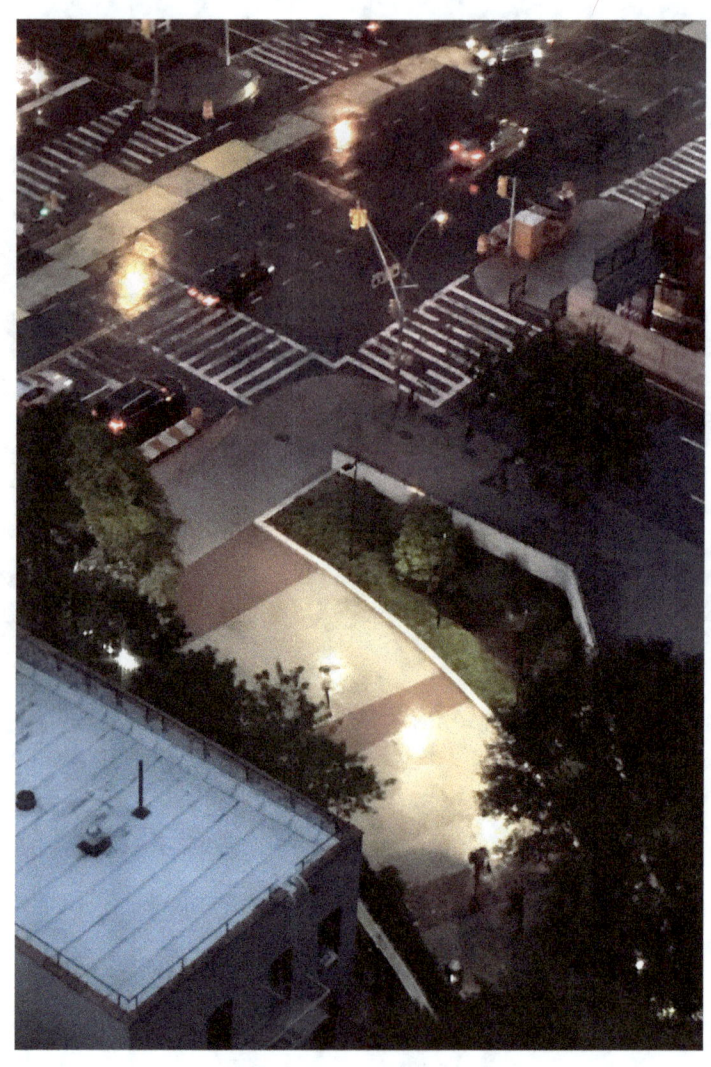

One Rainy Night. Photo. 2017.
Beautiful Bird's-eye view.
I was happy in that place, I was poor, though.

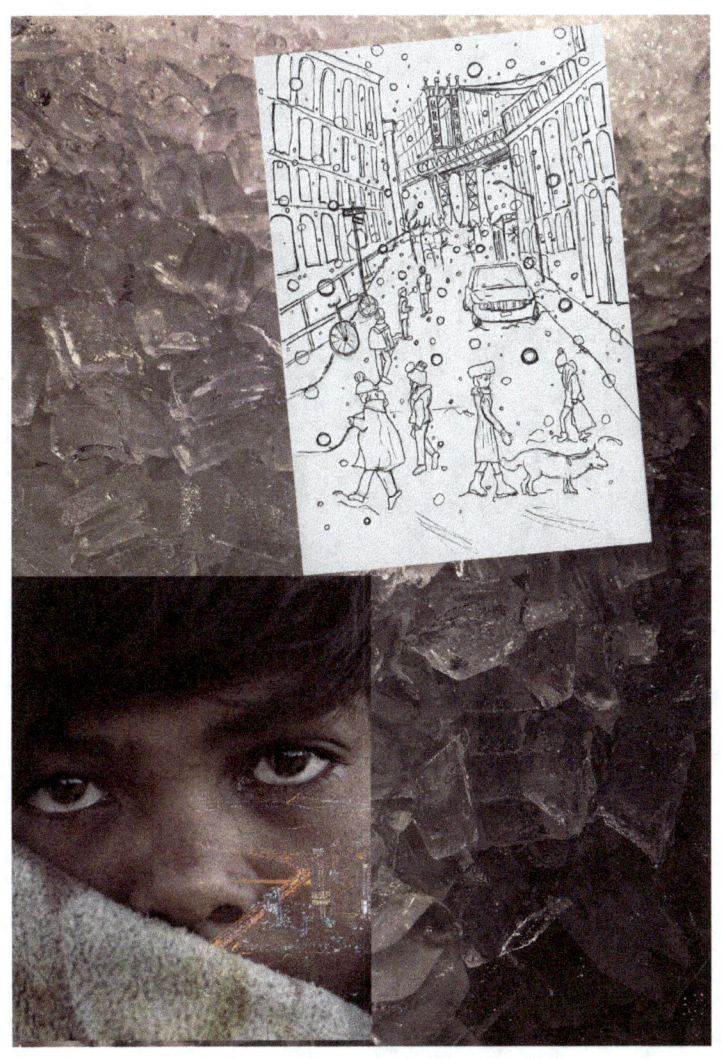

B-32. 2021.

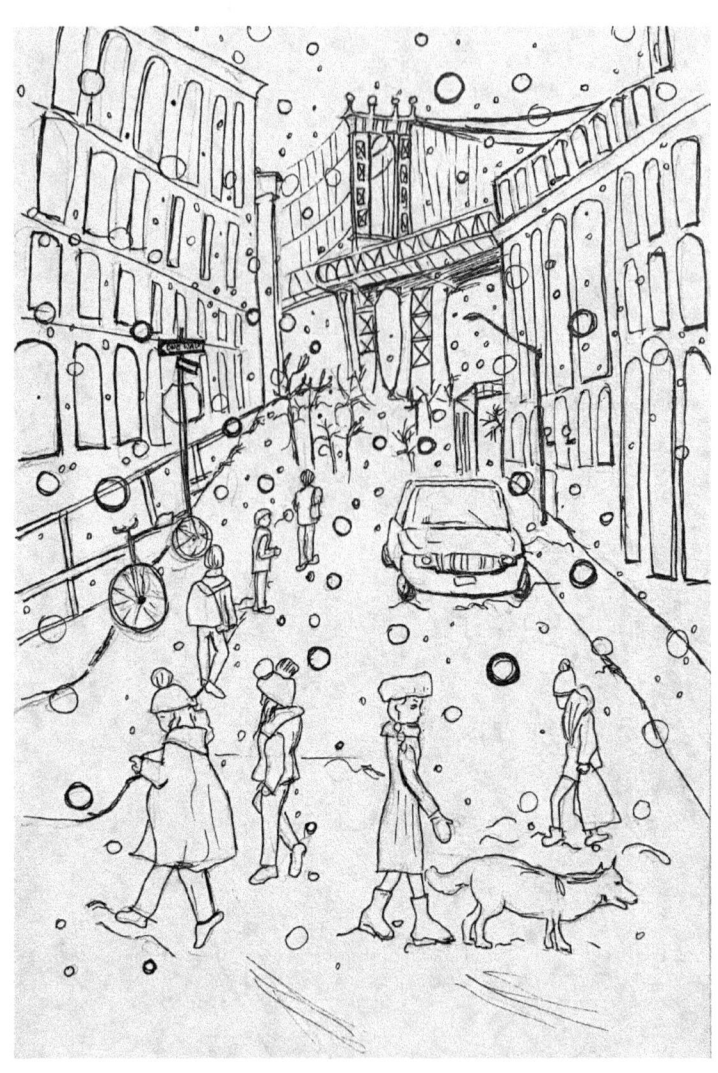

Snowing in NYC. Pen. 2020.
I love winter although
you always said that you were cold.

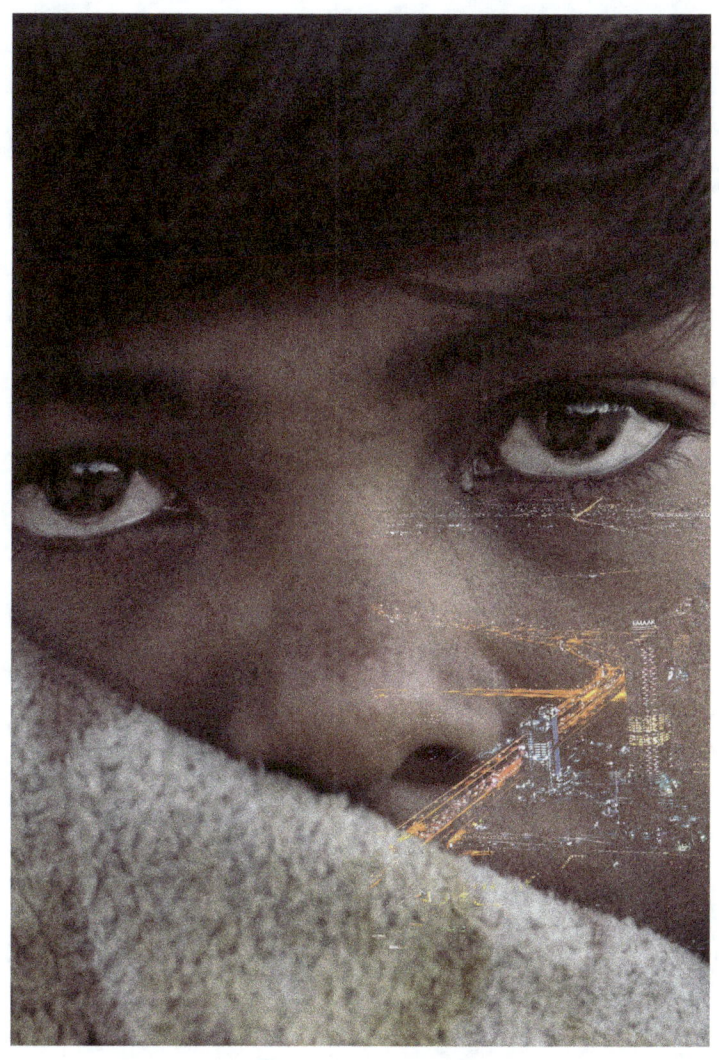

Fear of the war. Adobe Photoshop. 2019.
A boy holds a gun to me. I am watching you.

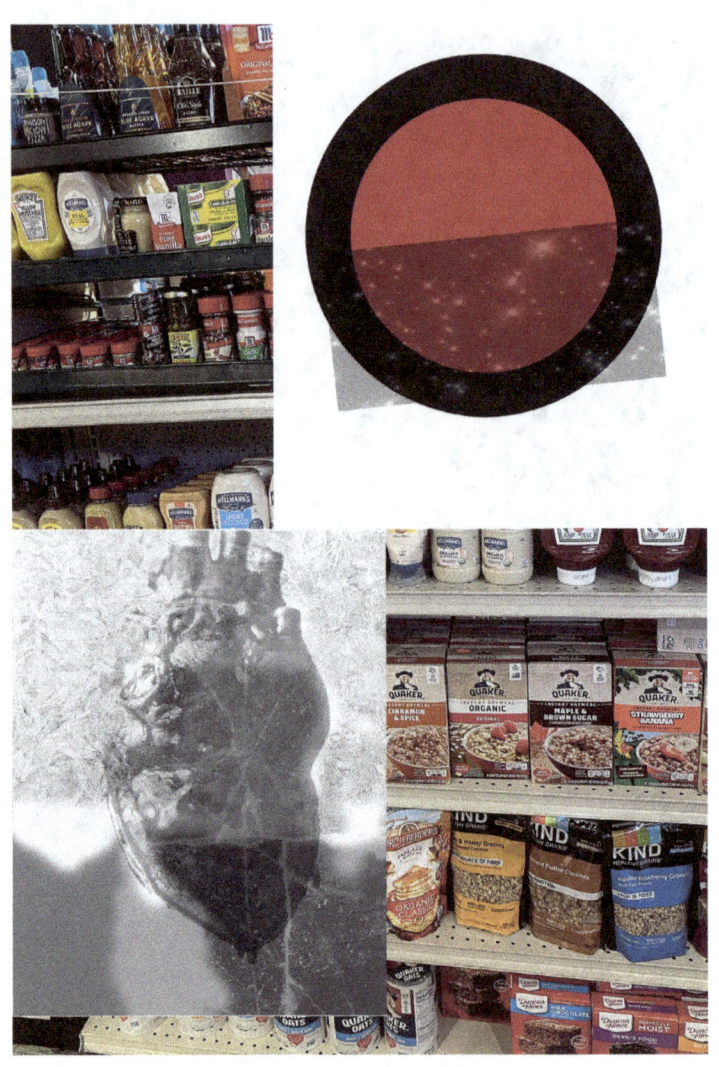

B-33. 2021.

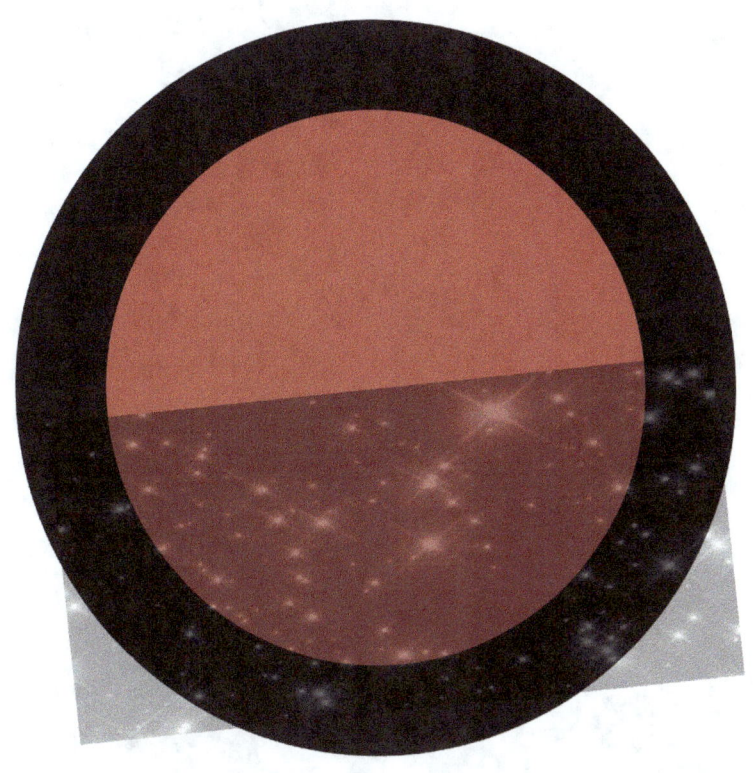

Sea. Adobe Photoshop. 2018.

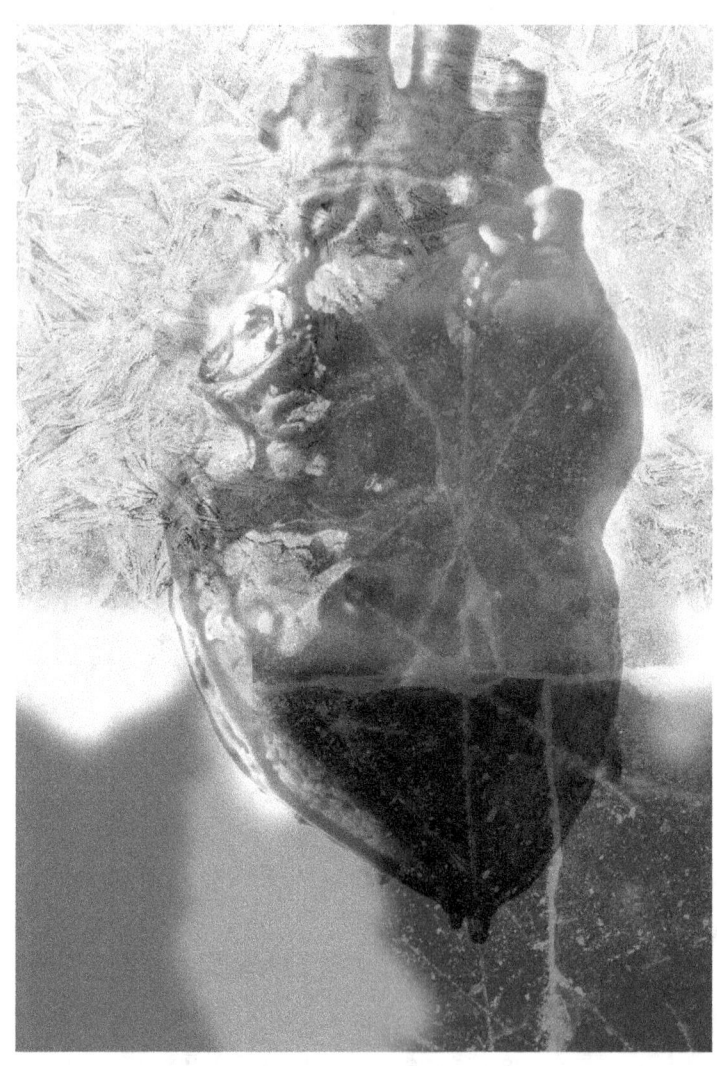

Frozen Heart. Adobe Photoshop. 2019.
This is mine. See how painful I am.

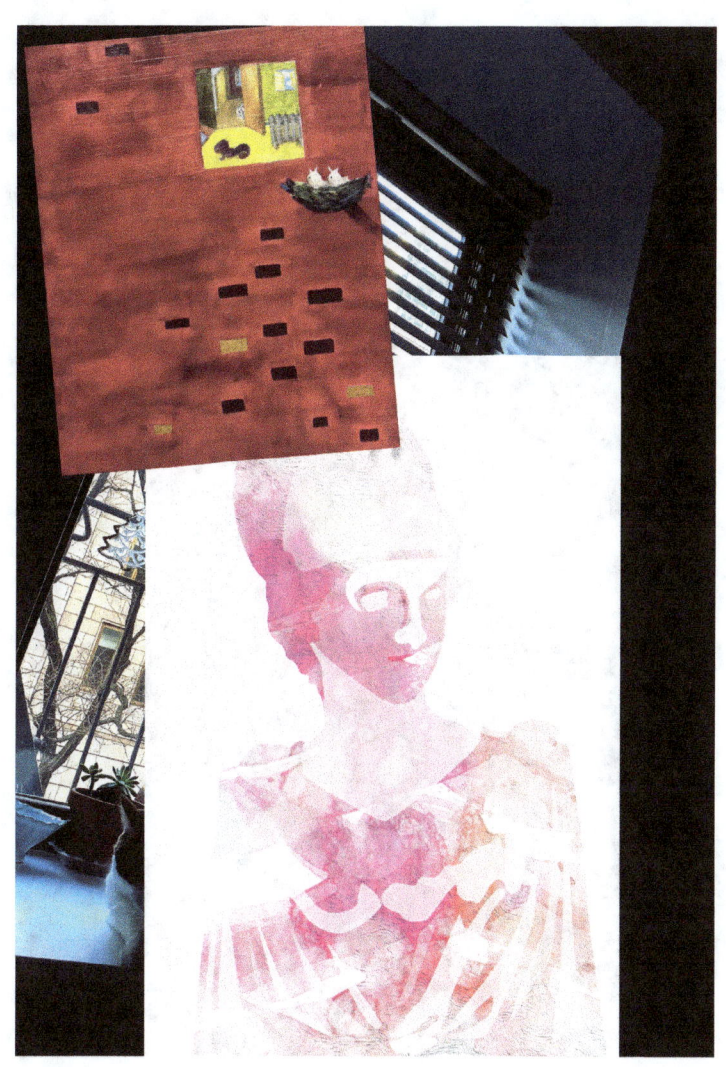

B-34. 2022.

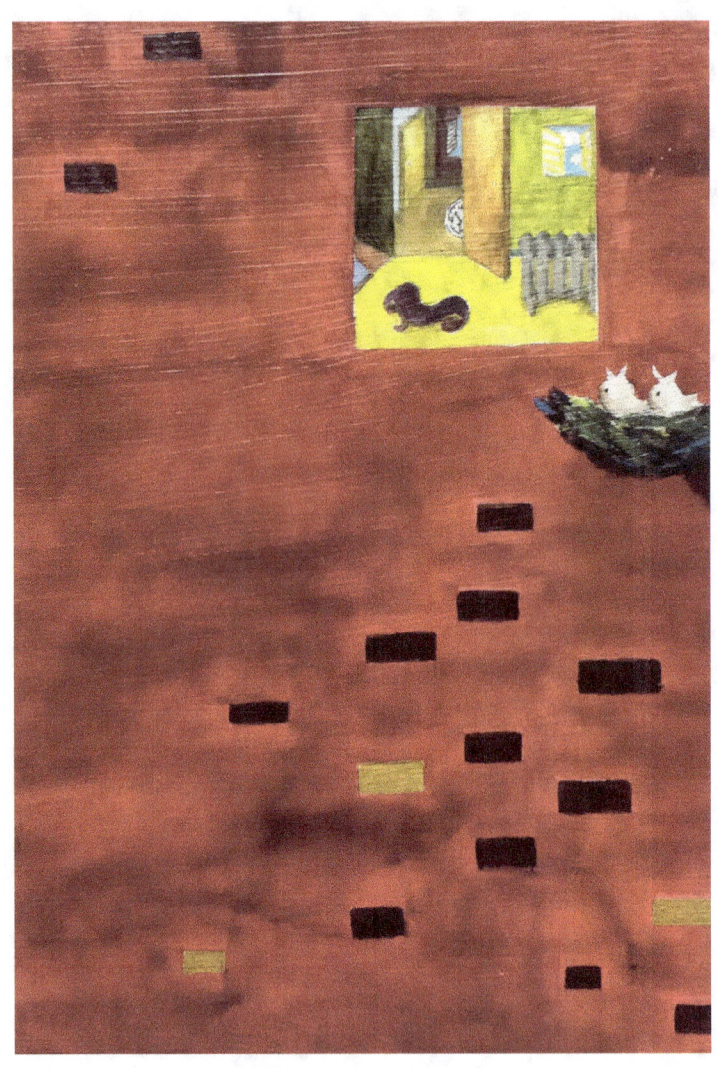

Tree House. Acrylic. 2014.

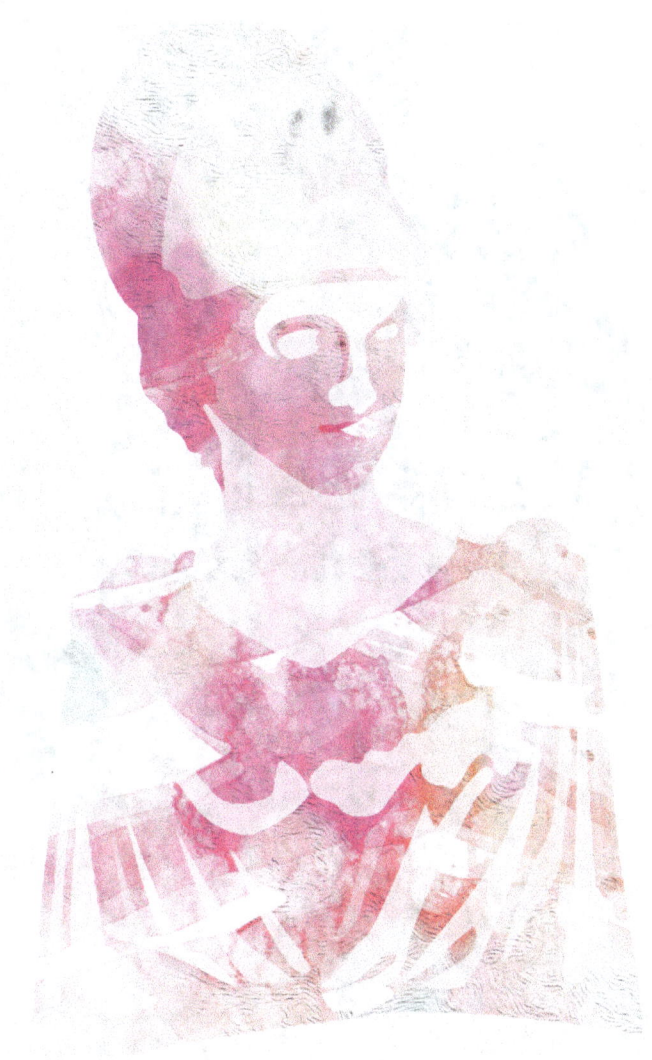

Minerva. Adobe Illustrator&Photoshop. 2022.
The goddess of wisdom, poetry, war, victory, medicine, and so forth. And strength!

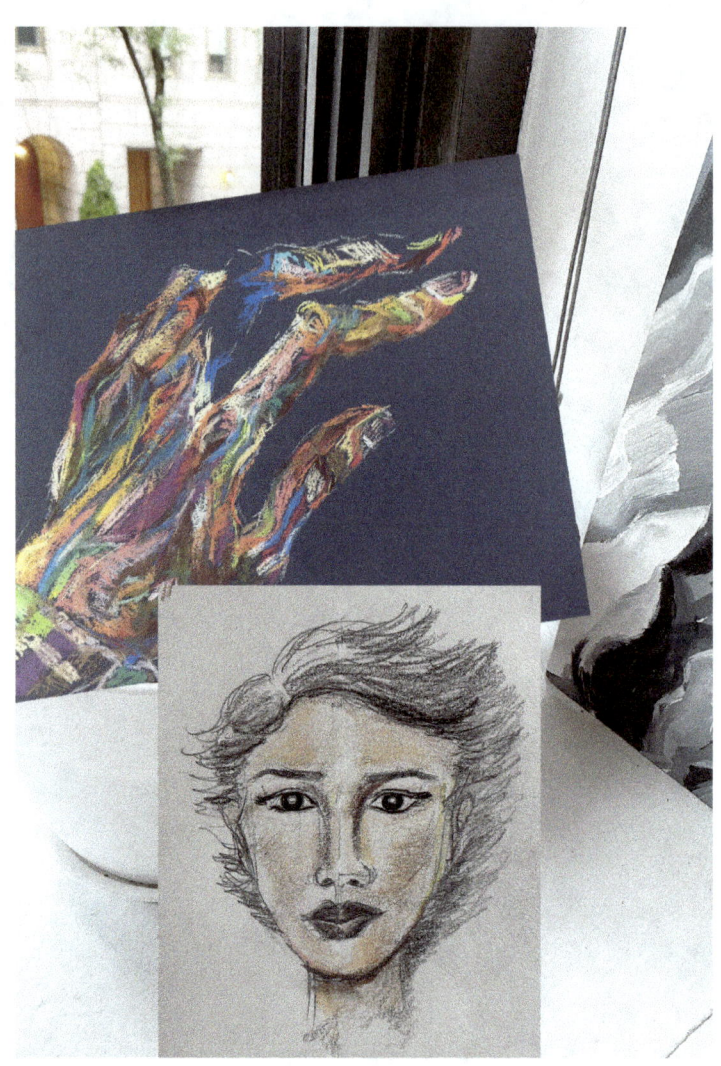

B-35. 2022.

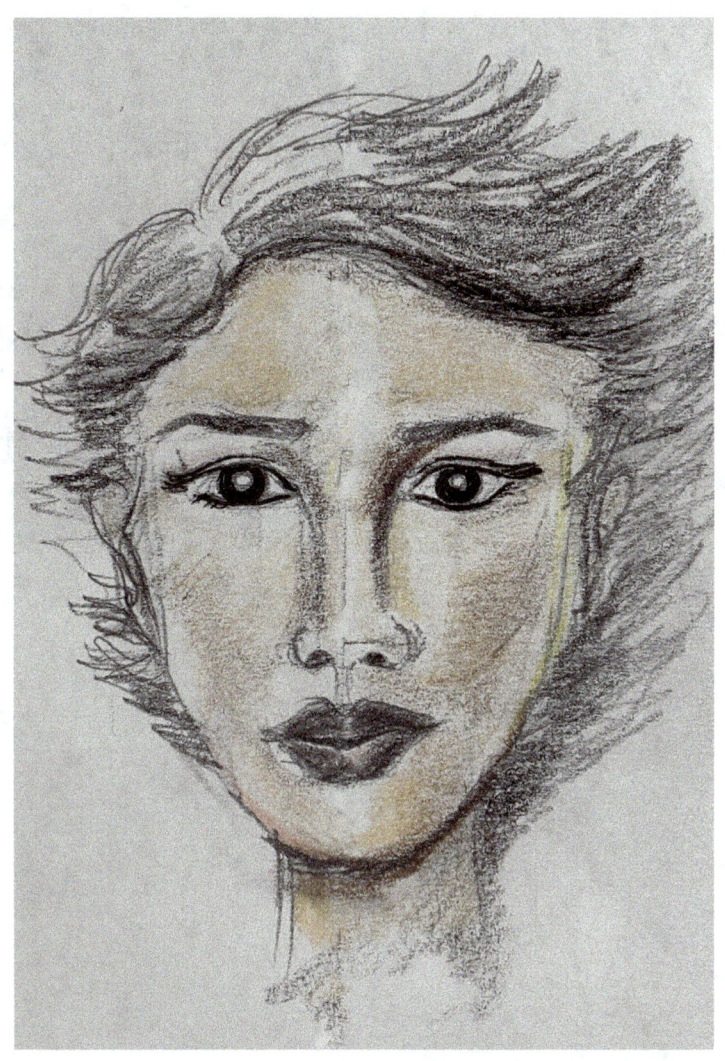

Untitled. Color Pencil. 2020.

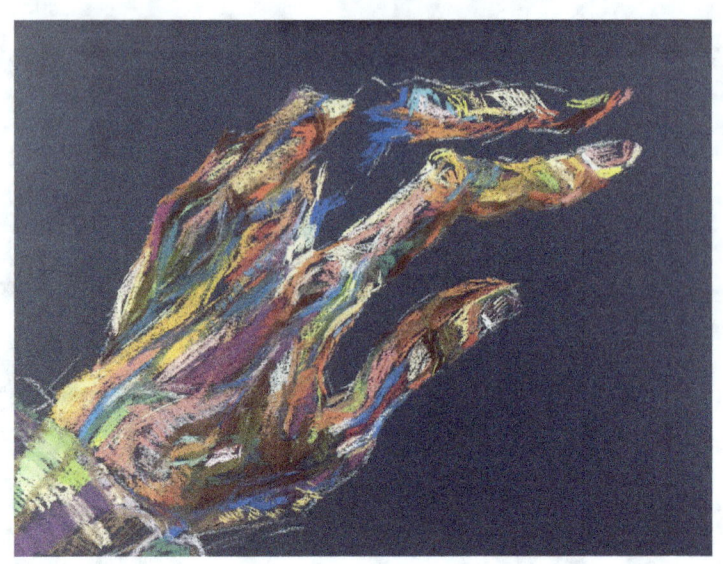

Hand. Pastel. 2016.

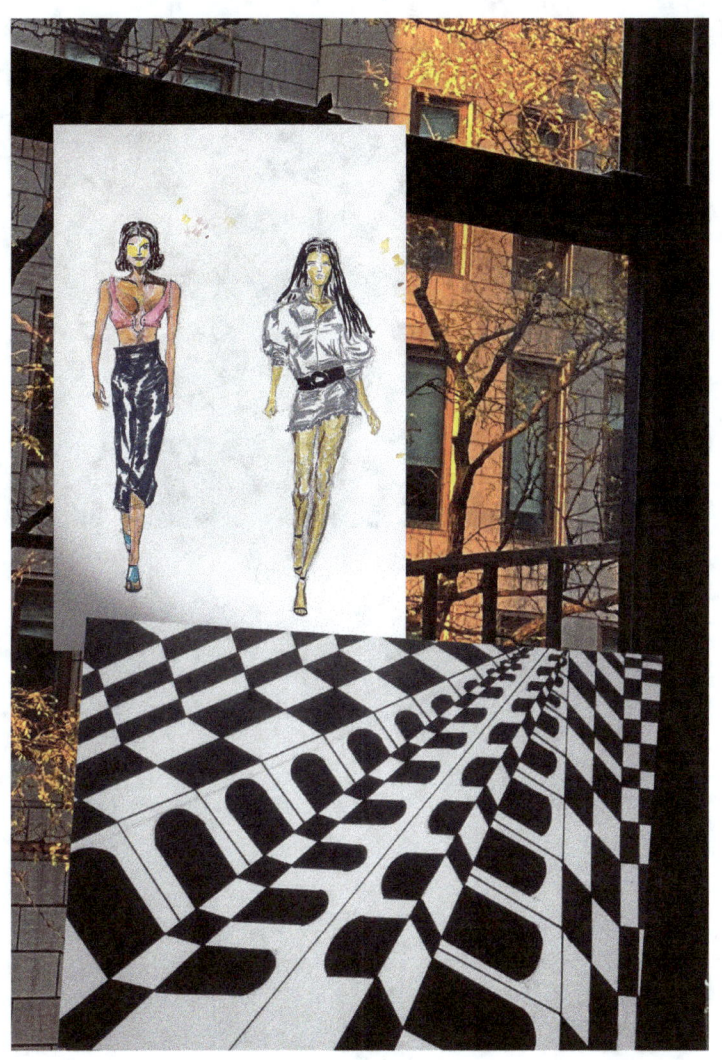

B-36. 2022.

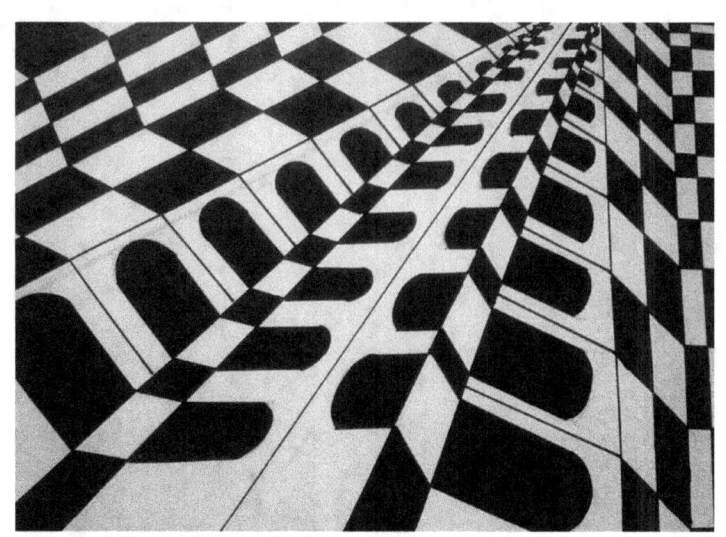

Untitled. Ink Pen. 2015.

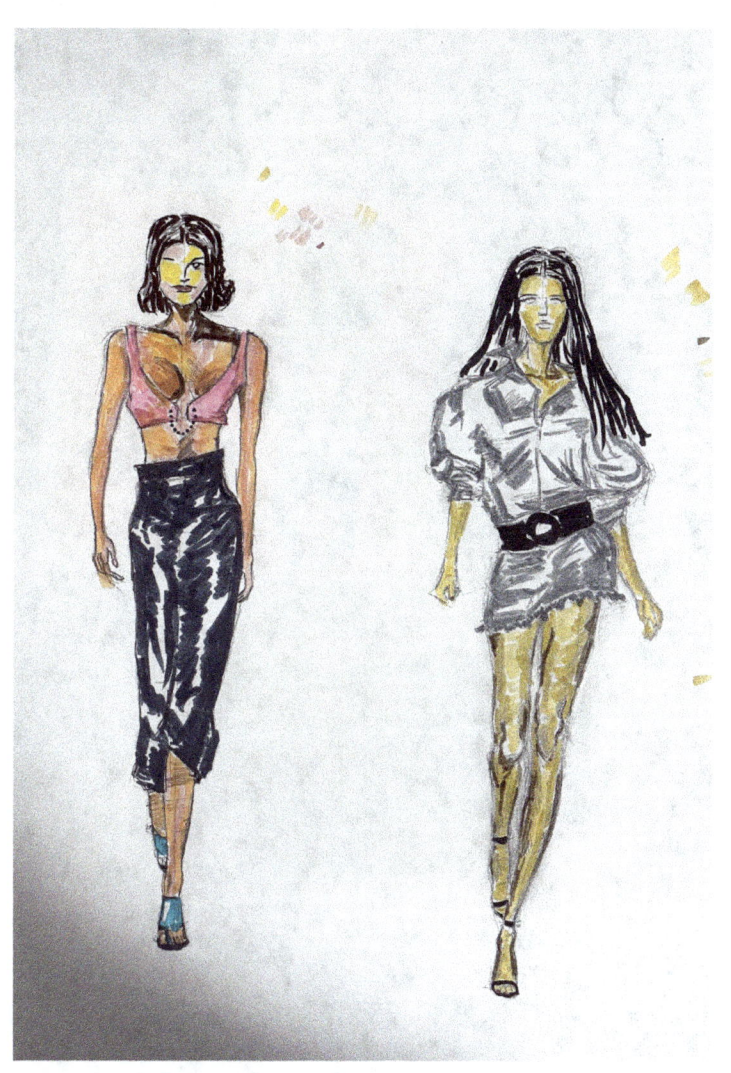

Untitled. Color Pen. 2020.

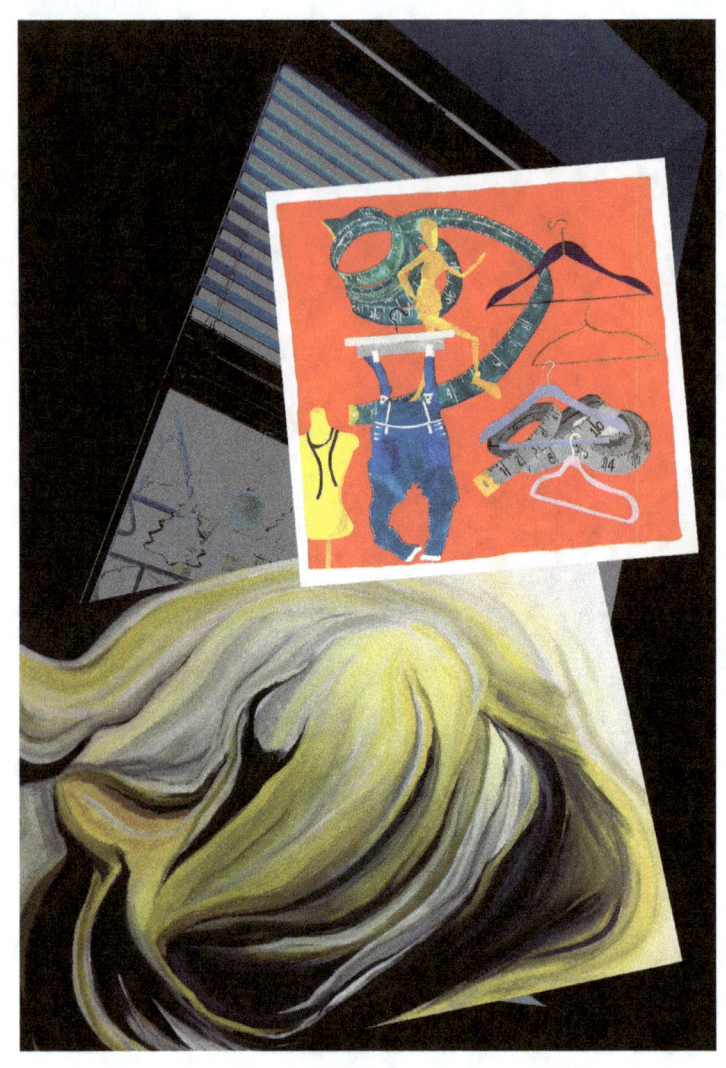

B-37. 2022.

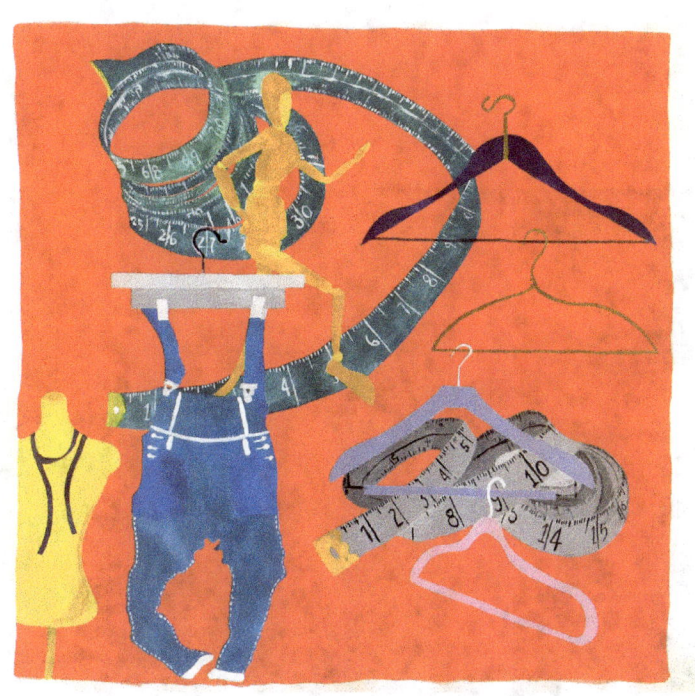

Scarf Design. Acrylic. 2016.

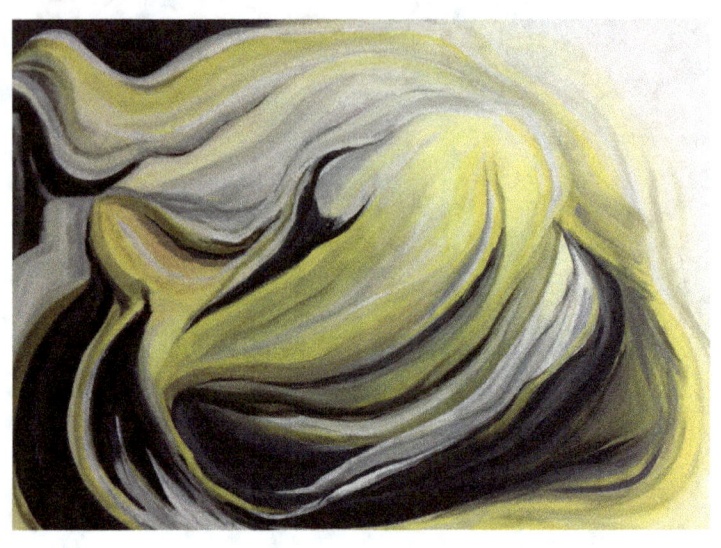

Untitled. Acrylic. 2014.

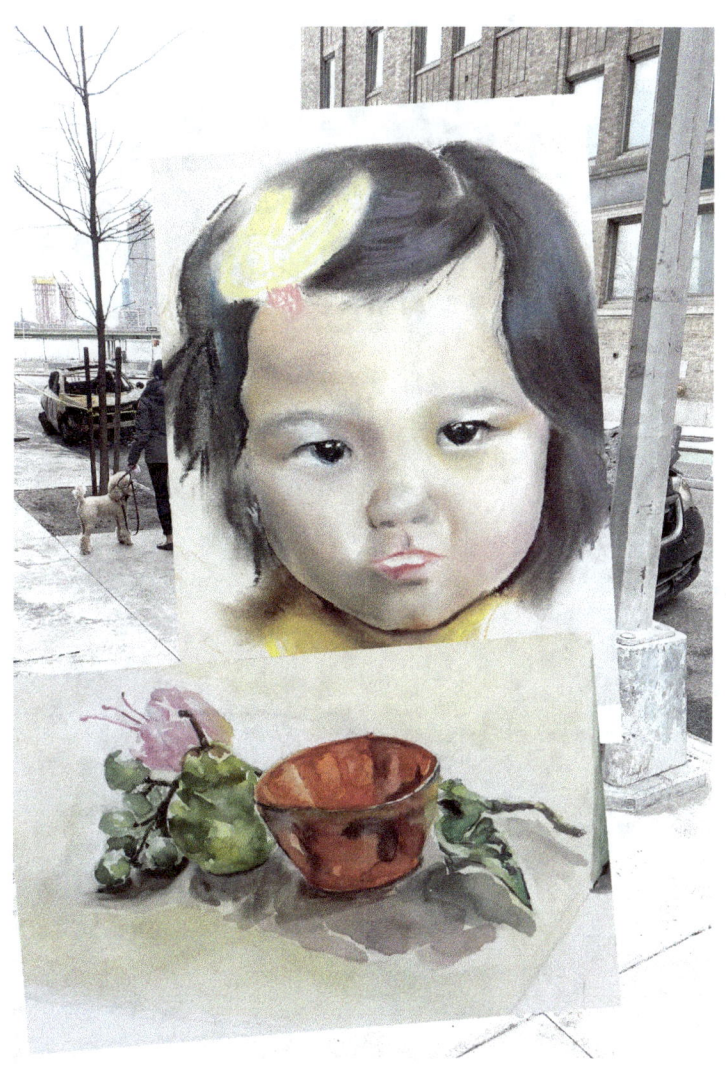

B-38. 2022.

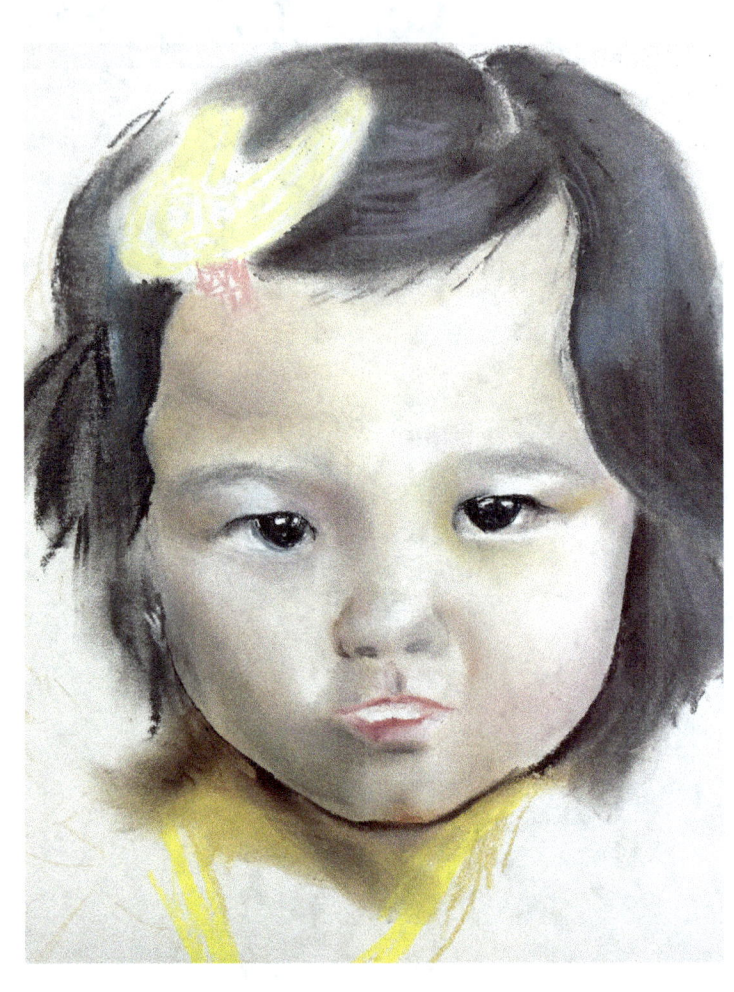

My girl. Pastel. 2015.
Be happy, my girl.

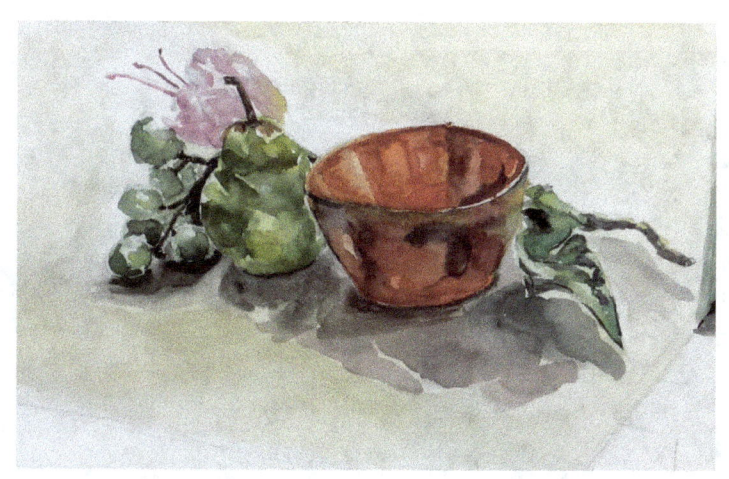

Still Life. Watercolor. 2015.

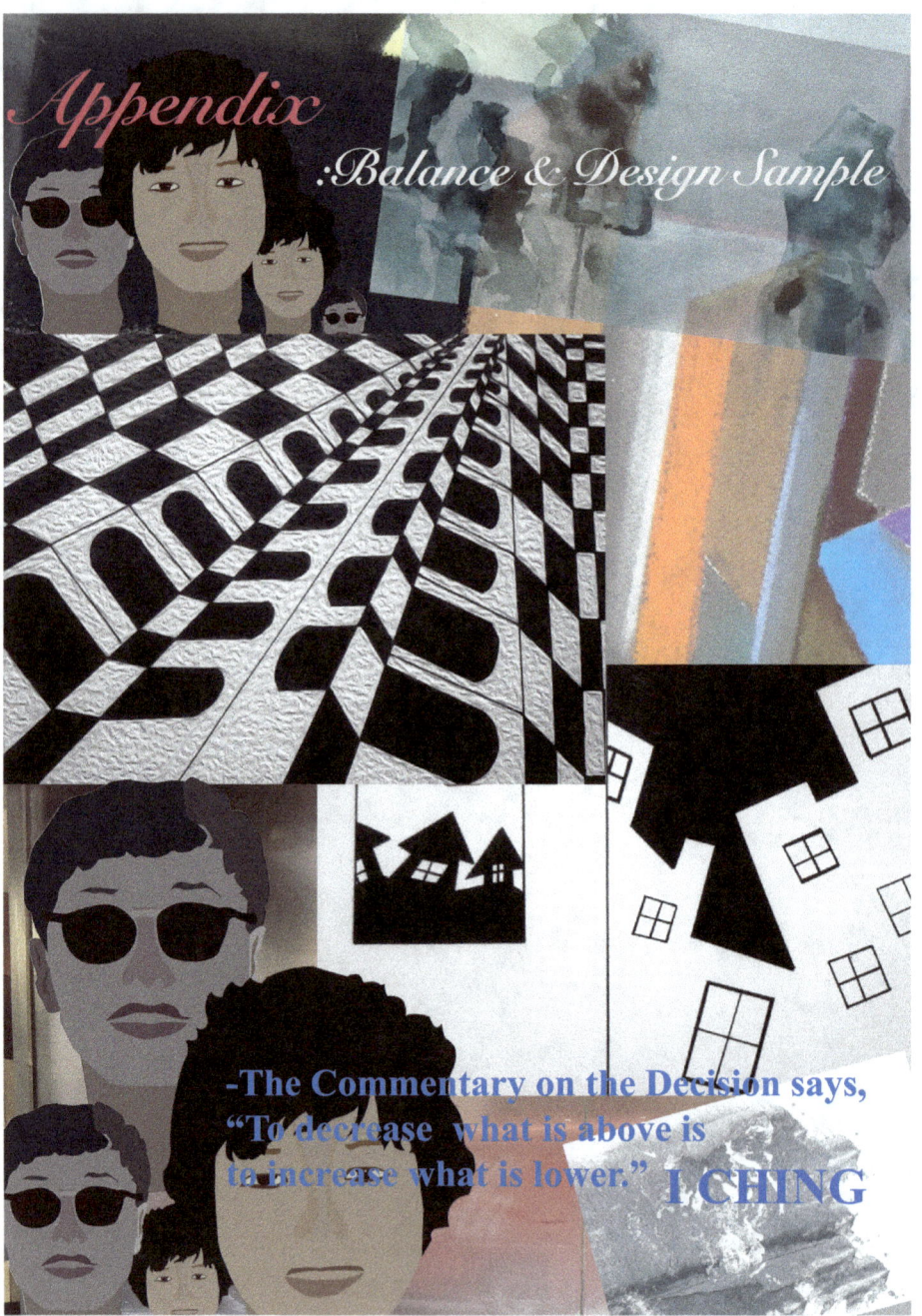

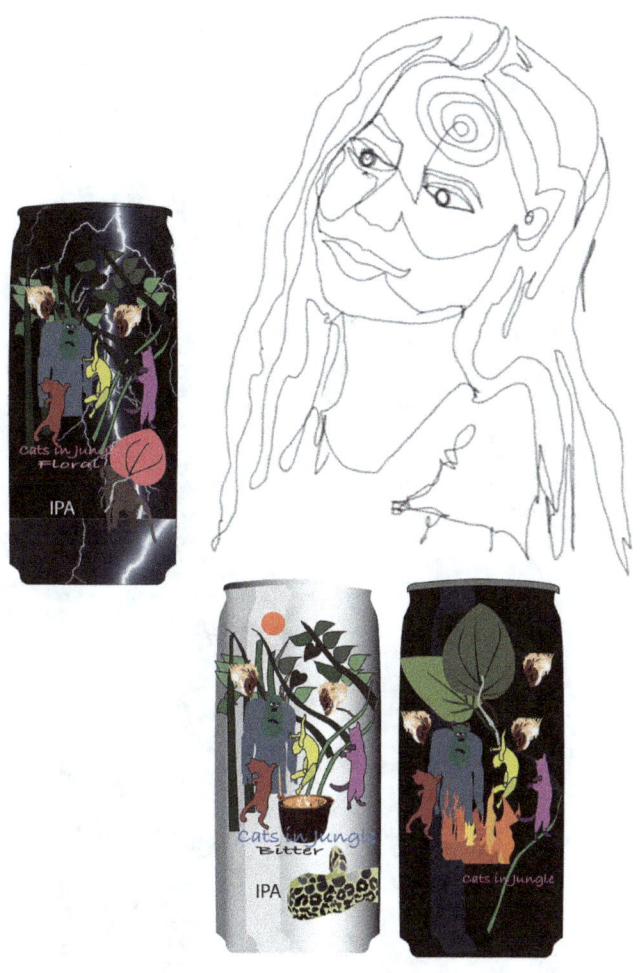

Adobe Photoshop. 2022.
Beer can design

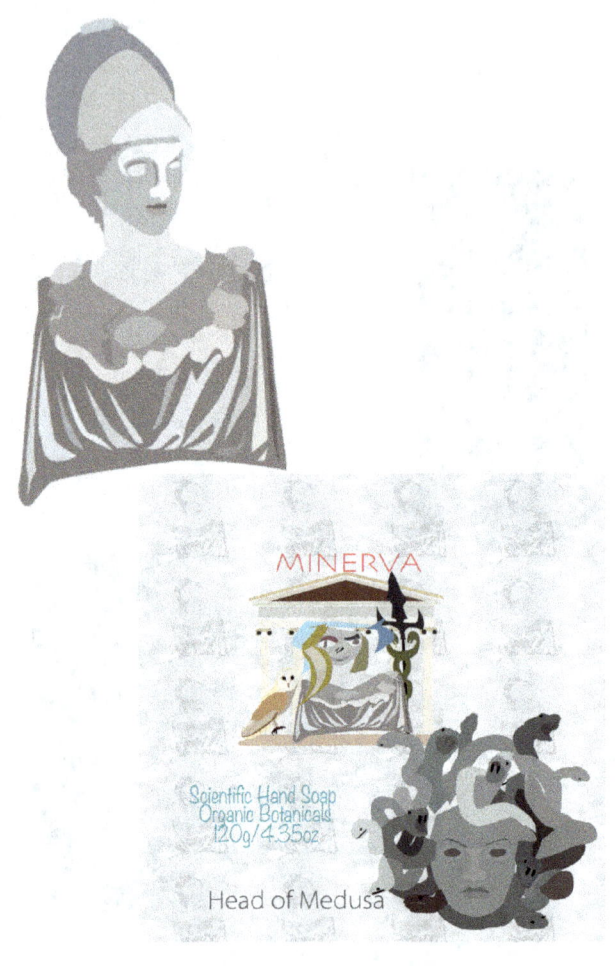

Adobe Illustrator & Photoshop. 2022.
Soap Package design

At the end

The completed artworks are finished by Adobe Photoshop, and the purpose of the study is to examine the balance. Some of individual pieces is available as a physical form, but most of those remains on a computer or a phone like memories in my brain. That is another purpose of this book, and it is the song for the memories without the body.

Thank you,

Moon-J, 2022.

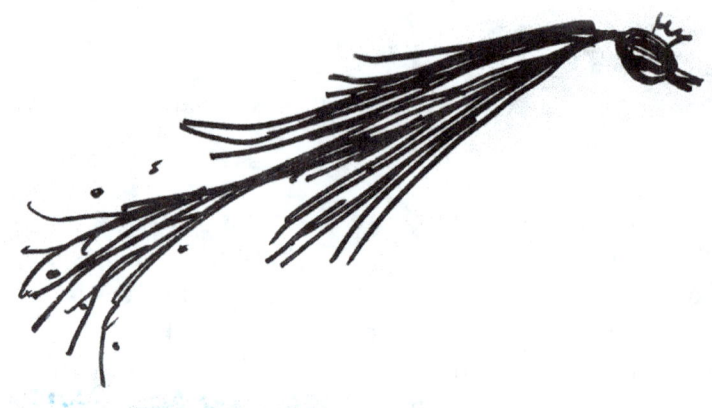

About the author

Moon-J
named
after
her
mother and father received Healthcare degree
as well as Fine Arts.
She currently lives in NYC.

www.ingramcontent.com/pod-product-compliance
Lightning Source LLC
Chambersburg PA
CBHW071419210526
45465CB00001B/460